OPPORTUNITIES IN ANIMATION AND CARTOONING CAREERS

Terence J. Sacks

Foreword by
Barry Young
Senior Faculty, Animation Program Director
Columbia College, Chicago

VGM Career Horizons
NTC/Contemporary Publishing Group

Library of Congress Cataloging-in-Publication Data

Sacks, Terence J.
    Opportunities in animation and cartooning careers / Terence J. Sacks.
       p.   cm. — (VGM opportunities series)
    Includes bibliographical references.
    ISBN 0-658-00182-5 (cloth) — ISBN 0-658-00183-3 (pbk.)
      1. Animation (Cinematography)—Vocational guidance—United States. 2.
Cartooning—Vocational guidance—United States. I. Title. II. Series.
NC1765 .S23 2000   99-089626
741.5'023'73—dc21   CIP

Cover photograph: © Columbia College, Chicago, IL

Published by VGM Career Horizons
A division of NTC/Contemporary Publishing Group, Inc.
4255 West Touhy Avenue, Lincolnwood (Chicago), Illinois 60712-1975 U.S.A.
Copyright © 2000 by NTC/Contemporary Publishing Group, Inc.
Printed in the United States of America
International Standard Book Number: 0-658-00182-5 (cloth)
                                            0-658-00183-3 (paper)

01 02 03 04 05 LB 15 14 13 12 11 10 9 8 7 6 5 4 3

CONTENTS

ABOUT THE AUTHOR

Terence J. Sacks is an independent writer-editor with more than twenty-five years of experience in communications. He has written dozens of news articles, magazine articles, and speeches as well as books. Sacks's articles have appeared in such publications as *LifeTimes, Hospitals,* and *Chicago Medicine.* He has written four books for VGM Career Horizons, including *Careers in Medicine, Careers in Nursing, Opportunities in Funeral Service Careers,* and *Opportunities in Physician Assistant Careers.*

A graduate of Northwestern's Medill School of Journalism, Sacks has strong credentials in health and medical topics. From 1970 to 1973 he was director of communications for the Chicago Medical Society, the local professional group for physicians in Chicago and Cook County. He has also held positions in communications for the American Osteopathic Association, the American Association of Dental Schools, and several hospitals in Chicago.

For the past fifteen years, Sacks has headed his own writing and communications firm, Terence J. Sacks Associates.

He is active in the Independent Writers of Chicago (on whose board he has served), the American Medical Writers Association, and the Publicity Club of Chicago.

FOREWORD

One of my earliest memories as a child was the Sunday morning ritual of reading the comics pages, then picking up a pencil or crayon and trying to emulate what I saw. I was lucky in that my parents, my mother in particular, encouraged me to draw. I recall vividly her dislike for coloring books, with outlined objects that you just filled in, and her insistence that I simply draw from memory and not worry how realistic it looked.

Children naturally like to draw. In fact, I spend a great deal of my time encouraging my college students to become more childlike in their approach to drawing and animating. It seems to me that creative thinking in any of the arts requires that you have a thorough understanding of yourself and your strengths and weaknesses before you can honestly express your creative thoughts and ideas.

As Mr. Sacks points out, today's youth are exposed to many more creative media tools than the basic paper-and-pencil techniques that many of us grew up with. Consequently, parents are faced with the difficult task of deciding which of these tools will truly help their children develop their artistic skills and expressive abilities, rather than simply entertain them. I advise parents to help their children focus on basic artistic skill development with pencil and paper, along with encouraging work on projects that involve thinking and working with their hands, such as with cut paper.

Mr. Sacks carefully traces the origin of cartoons, defines and discusses employment, and lays the groundwork for entering the profession of cartooning and animation, a profession filled with challenge and excitement. If you've grown up doodling and sketching and wishing you could actually make a living at it, I think you'll find that this book unlocks warm memories and answers the question, "Just where do cartoonists and animators come from?"

As Mr. Sacks explains, you can make a living at it; you'll just have to show great patience and persistence, and realize that preparation begins early in life. Raoul Servaise, the great Belgian animator, once said that an animator was much like God because of his power to create from a blank piece of paper.

What better way to make a living than to bring to life your ideas and drawings each day?

Barry Young
Senior Faculty, Animation Program Director
Columbia College, Chicago

CHAPTER 1

CARTOONING 101

If you are typical of most Americans, your grandparents grew up chuckling over cartoon strips, or the "funnies," as many of us call them, in the local daily and Sunday newspapers. Most of these folks will nostalgically tell you about the cartoon strips of their day: *L'il Orphan Annie, Dick Tracy, Blondie, Dennis the Menace, Peanuts, Gasoline Alley, Prince Valiant, Winnie Winkle, Tillie the Toiler, Smilin' Jack,* and *Smokey Stover,* to name but a few. Many of these have long since passed into oblivion. A few are still around, although their originators may have passed on. No doubt about it—the comics, funnies, cartoon strips, whatever you may call them, have entertained generations of readers, and are perhaps as popular, or more popular, than they have ever been.

A POPULAR PASTIME

A survey commissioned by Metropolitan Sunday Newspapers several years ago showed that more than 86 million of us read the Sunday comics at least once every four weeks. The study showed further that nearly half of the newspaper readers felt that the comics contributed greatly to their enjoyment of the Sunday newspaper, and three-quarters of them said that reading the comics is a good way to introduce reading the newspaper to children. Nine out of ten readers in this survey agreed that comics help and encourage children to learn how to read.

In another recent poll, the ten most popular comics for all adults (18 to 55) were *Calvin and Hobbes, Blondie, Garfield, The Far Side, Peanuts, Doonesbury, For Better or for Worse, Beetle Bailey, Family Circus,* and *Cathy.* Since the survey was conducted, three of these cartoons are no longer syndicated—the cartoonists have either retired or gone on to other cartooning options. These are *Calvin and Hobbes, The Far Side,* and *Doonesbury.* Comic strips that rated tops with younger readers were much the same except for the addition of three new strips: *The Born Loser, Marvin,* and *Hi and Lois* in place of *Beetle Bailey, Doonesbury,* and *For Better or for Worse.* The poll also found that of adults 18 to 34 with household incomes of $35,000 or more, 57 percent read the Sunday comics. Of adults age 25 to 54, 58 percent read comics. And 47 percent of mothers age 18 to 34 read the comics with their children.

Clearly, the comics are read and enjoyed by millions of newspaper readers, and they have a great impact on their readers. In a 1995 survey, the *Chicago Tribune* received responses from 17,000 readers as to the cartoon strips they read and found interesting. As you might have guessed, many of the strips that made the *Tribune*'s most-popular list were the same as those found on the other survey, including *The Far Side, Calvin and Hobbes, Peanuts, Beetle Bailey, Blondie,* and *For Better or for Worse.* Not only did 17,000 *Tribune* readers take the time to fill out the survey, but thousands enclosed letters, complaints, suggestions, and even portfolios of their own cartoons. The unmistakable message to *Tribune* editors: "Do not mess around with our comics!"

When Bill Watterson, creator of the extremely popular cartoon strip *Calvin and Hobbes,* decided to call it quits in 1998, the howls of anguish from readers was almost unbelievable. Earlier that year, Gary Larson, creator of *The Far Side,* had decided to retire. Following the demise of *Calvin and Hobbes,* one reader, a professor of popular culture at an Ohio college, wrote, "The end of *Calvin and Hobbes* is a disaster. We need *Cathy* to whine about her bathing suit every spring, we need Dagwood to make his giant sandwiches, and Charlie Brown to fall down kicking the football...these comic strips bring stability to our lives...Bill Watterson has no right to do this to us...."

Nevertheless, Watterson's decision is not so strange. It takes a lot of hard work to come up with the ideas and inspiration to create a comic strip day in and day out, 365 days a year. That such veteran cartoonists as recently retired Charles M. Schulz, creator of *Peanuts,* Hank Ketcham, creator of *Dennis the Menace,* and Mort Walker, creator of *Beetle Bailey,* have endured as long as they have is not only proof of their versatility and talent but of their endurance—not to mention their ability to strike a responsive chord among millions of readers all over the United States and Canada.

THE ROCKY ROAD TO SUCCESS

Cartooning is a highly lucrative and rewarding business for the vast majority of newspaper comic strip artists who are syndicated—in other words, whose cartoon strip appears in hundreds of newspapers in Canada and the United States. Syndicated cartoonists can earn hundreds of thousands of dollars yearly, depending on the number and size of the papers in which the comic strip appears. But while surveys can track the popularity of cartoons and comic strips like *Calvin and Hobbes,* what they cannot show is that nearly every successful cartoonist struggles for years, receiving numerous rejections of his or her work, before gaining recognition in the field.

Take *Tumbleweeds* creator Tom Ryan. While creating editorial and sports cartoons for a local newspaper, Ryan held a variety of jobs in order to support his growing family. Eventually, he landed a job at the bottom of the commercial art ladder. It wasn't a glamorous job, but it was a living, and through it he gained a working ability in cartooning. He also took an art correspondence course. Through his commercial art experience, he cultivated several art and cartooning styles and eventually developed the particular style he used to create *Tumbleweeds,* one of the most popular cartoon strips of all time. *Family Circus*'s Bill Keane had a solid foundation of freelancing behind him before achieving success. He was thirty-eight years old before starting *Family Circus,* had worked as a staff artist for the *Philadelphia Bulletin* for fifteen years, and had drawn freelance cartoons for major magazines. Bud Grace, creator of the syndicated cartoon strip *Ernie,* intended to be a doctor and was thirty-eight before he even began drawing cartoons. It took him eight years to sell his first gag cartoon to the *Saturday Review.* As time went on, he sold more and more to magazines. Eventually, he submitted sample strips of *Ernie* to King Features and they bought it.

Similar stories of struggle and adversity can be told by almost every successful cartoonist today. So unless you truly want to work as a cartoonist and accept that it will most likely take many years to hit the big time, you are probably better off forgetting about cartooning as a career.

JUST WHAT IS A CARTOON, ANYWAY?

Put simply, a cartoon is a drawing or a series of drawings that tells a story or imparts a message, usually of a humorous nature. Sometimes, though, cartoons are serious and thought provoking. Many of Bill Mauldin's cartoons during World War II were grim, telling of the incredible hardships our men in combat had to confront. Cartoonists usually communicate their messages through a combination of words and drawings, but sometimes they choose to express themselves through drawings alone. Many great cartoons are almost childlike in their simplicity. The objective may be to entertain, teach, or express an opinion about a person, event, or current events.

When the cartoonist is attempting to satirize, poke fun, or lampoon some person or persons, he or she seldom draws objects as they are in real life. The drawing most often exaggerates some feature of the subject, such as the head, nose, eyebrows, hands, or feet. Such exaggeration is called caricature. For example, the human head is about an eighth of the length of the body, but in a cartoon, the head of a character may be a third of the body's entire length. This helps the cartoonist focus on distinctive features and expressions—a sneer or a smile or an angry squint.

Cartoons can be split into five basic groups, each offering special challenges and requiring special skills: editorial or political cartoons; comic strips, panels, and comic books; gag or magazine cartoons; humorous or illustrative cartoons; and animated cartoons, which like live-action films are projected onto a screen.

Editorial or Political Cartoons

The editorial cartoon tries to do with drawings what newspaper editorials do in words. Featured primarily in newspapers and magazines as a single drawing with or without captions, the editorial cartoon tries to persuade readers to adopt an opinion about some timely political issue. Such cartoons are often directly relevant to a particular event in the news.

Editorial cartoonists often use a particular symbol to help convey their meaning quickly and simply. For instance, one of the greatest American cartoonists, Thomas Nast, drew a ferocious tiger representing Tammany Hall, the corrupt New York City political machine, attacking a beautiful young girl representing the innocent public lying helpless on the ground. Nast also introduced the elephant as the long-standing and recognized symbol of the Republican party, and the donkey as the hallmark of the Democratic party.

The work of political cartoonists is powerful enough to rate a special category among the Pulitzer prize awards. Winners in recent years include Herbert L. Block (who signs his cartoons as "Herblock"), Bill Mauldin, and John Fischetti.

Comic Strips, Panels, and Comic Books

Comic strips and panels regularly appear in newspapers and magazines, and the content and tone of these comics are as varied as their readers. Some, like *Dick Tracy,* originated by the late Chester Gould, are adventure strips that continue their stories from day to day. Others, like Johnny Hart's *B.C.* and Charles M. Schulz's *Peanuts,* are discrete from day to day, and written in a humorous vein. A large metropolitan daily may print a page or two of cartoons and comic strips every day.

Cartoons also appear in magazine form as comic books and may feature a single story, a collection of stories, or a continuous story. Comic books may feature adventure or fantasy stories, like *Spider Man* or *Superman,* or humorous themes, such as *Peanuts* or *Archie.* With hundreds of titles in existence, comic books remain one of the biggest and most lucrative venues for artists with cartooning skills. Comic book creators Frank Miller and Alex Ross have revolutionized the comic book industry by converting the books from a medium primarily aimed at youngsters to one that attracts many adult readers. Miller's four-part comic book series *Batman: The Dark Knight Returns* sold an impressive 250,000 copies, and the hardcover version made the *New York Times* bestseller list. Ross's realistic paintings have made him one of the most sought-after comic books artists today, with his work appearing in both Marvel and DC Comics, two of the leaders in the comic book field.

Gag or Magazine Cartoons

Gag cartoons are printed primarily in magazines, such as the *New Yorker* and *Playboy,* and feature single-panel drawings with a one-line caption. Newspapers sometimes print several gag cartoons throughout the newspaper, on the comic pages or elsewhere, perhaps on pages that have nothing but classified ads. Gag cartoons like Brad Anderson's

Marmaduke enjoy great popularity with many newspaper readers.

Gag cartoons amuse the reader by poking fun not only at a specific person, but also at people in general. Some of the great magazine cartoonists have entertained readers by satirizing human flaws. A few of the great comic satirists are the late James Thurber, Helen Hokinson, and Charles Addams, whose morbid but funny cartoons appeared for years in the *New Yorker.* Addams's cartoons inspired the highly popular TV series *The Munsters.*

Illustrative Cartoons

Illustrative cartoons help to explain or illuminate stories, textbooks, or advertisements. While they may convey little meaning in themselves, they do help underscore the message of the text they accompany. Examples of highly successful book cartoonists are the Berenstains (of Berenstein Bears fame), the late Shel Silverstein, and of course the incomparable Dr. Seuss, whose illustrated books have sold in the hundreds of millions.

Animated Cartoons

The final category of cartooning is animation, a technique by which filmmakers use cartoons to create the illusion of motion (animation means "to give motion" or "life"). The filmmaker photographs a series of drawings one frame at a time. The position of the drawings varies minutely from frame to frame, but when run through a projector, the subjects appear to move. Animation employing computers has been used successfully by George Lucas, creator of the *Star Wars* films, and others to create and bring to life dozens of fantastic creatures. These creatures move, act, and speak as if they were three-dimensional characters.

Outside the film industry, animation can be found in a variety of diverse fields. Animation is often used by advertisers to highlight and sell their product, as in the popular series of polar bear commercials by Budweiser beer. It is featured in video and computer games produced by the likes of Nintendo and Sega—this is one of the most rapidly growing segments of the cartoon industry. Instructional film producers often use animation to explain a technique or concept that may not be readily conveyed through live action.

THE MARKETPLACE

As a cartoonist you have many options to choose from in applying your talents to a unique and satisfying career. You may choose to illustrate books, create characters for advertising agencies, or put your career in motion with animation. Look around you to find interesting avenues that few may consider, like illustrating greeting cards—one of the most fertile fields for employment.

In recent years, the newspaper industry has diminished as a leading employer of political, comic strip, and gag cartoonists. The number of daily newspapers has declined from a high of 2,200 published in 1910 to about 1,500 published today. As a result, the number of spots open for cartoon strips and political cartoons has also decreased and the competition is fiercer than ever. This does not mean that there are no jobs available. Newspapers and syndicates, which supply most of the strips featured by newspapers, are always on the lookout for a cartoon whose style is unique and distinctive, like Gary Larson's wildly successful *The Far Side* or Mort Walker's *Beetle Bailey.* If you have a fresh idea and a lot of talent, you can make it as the creator of a cartoon strip.

The proof of the pudding is *The Boondocks,* a cartoon strip that made its national debut in May 1999 in 195 cities throughout the country. The strip first appeared in creator Aaron McGruder's campus newspaper at the University of Maryland. It seeks to attract younger readers with its references to hip-hop and its candid discussion of race, according to an article featured in *Time* magazine. The strip deals with "racial issues which are still alive and festering beneath the rug of polite society," according to McGruder. Although previously unknown, the twenty-five-year-old artist reportedly signed a six-figure contract.

Syndication

If you create cartoons for newspapers or magazines, there is always the possibility that your strip or panel will be picked up by a syndicate, as was the case with *The Boondocks.* There are several major syndicates in the United States (see Appendix D) that will attempt to sell a cartoonist's product to any number of newspapers and magazines. You get paid a certain amount for each paper to which the syndicate succeeds in selling your strip. The scope of the distribution of each paper and the number of papers that pick up your strip determine what you are paid. Quite often, this can amount to a very tidy sum. In recent years, however, syndication as a moneymaker for cartoonists has taken second place to two fast-growing major markets—comic books and animation.

The Lucrative Field of Comic Books

Today there are more comic books than ever. Why? One of the comic book's major attractions is the opportunity it affords cartoonists to stretch their imagination and creativity. Comic books have printed stories ranging from Mozart's opera *The Magic Flute* to *Maus,* a survivor's diary of the Holocaust, which renders the Jews as mice and the Nazis as fanged cats. The money is good too. Experienced writers often earn more than $1,000 for a comic book; doing three or four books a month produces a nice income.

A Bright Future in Animation

While there are some depressions in the overall market for cartoonists, the future is especially bright for those with the unique skills required of animators. This fast-growing field is undergoing a revolution fueled in part by high-tech wizards armed with graphics software and high-powered work stations. Animated films were once populated solely by fetching beauties and ferocious beasts, all drawn lovingly, if somewhat tediously, by hand. That ended in 1995 with the release of *Toy Story,* the first computer-driven feature film and the only animated film to approach $200 million at the box office since 1994's Disney epic *The Lion King.*

Subsequently, the overwhelming popularity of cartoons like Pixar's *A Bug's Life* and DreamWorks' *Antz* suggests there will soon be a barrage of films created with computer graphics imaging, also known as CGI. Even as this is written, Pixar is hard at work on the release of *Toy Story 2* and DreamWorks is finishing a project titled *Shrek,* which deals with the creatures lurking beneath a child's bed. In addition, Universal is proceeding with *Frankenstein,* created by George Lucas's Industrial Light and Magic, and Warner Bros. is readying to release *The Iron Giant,* the tale of a machine that befriends a boy in Maine in the 1950s.

Even though, in feature film, traditional cel-generated animation seems to be on the decline, most films are still produced through a combination of cel animation and computer graphics imaging. Disney's *Tarzan* and *Fantasia 2000* rely on traditional animation but also feature large doses of computer-created elements. In DreamWorks' *Prince of Egypt,* over half of the shots contain computer-driven effects. The seven-minute parting of the Red Sea scene, for example, required ten digital artists, a two-dimension artist, sixteen traditional animators, and two programmers. It took 318,000 computer rendering hours to produce 600,000 digitally generated refugees for the scene. Imagine how long it would have taken traditional cel animators to painstakingly produce these seven minutes of film!

And that's not the end of the story. Thanks to Fox TV's *The Simpsons* and Comedy Central's tremendously successful *South Park,* networks including Fox, UPN (United Paramount Network), and Warner Bros. launched seven new prime-time cartoons created by traditional cel animation in the 1999–2000 season. Fox led the pack with three cartoon sitcoms: *The PJ's,* starring Eddie Murphy, Seth McFarlane's *Family Guy,* and the eagerly anticipated *Futurama* from Matt Groening, creator of *The Simpsons.* In the words of Fox's programming chief, who is responsible for the network's animated shockumentaries *(World's Deadliest Swarms, When Pets Go Bad),* viewers can "find live-action sitcoms elsewhere. They don't have to come here for them." Even as Fox replenishes its animation stock, UPN is readying *Dilbert,* based on the immensely popular cartoon strip dealing with corporate madness, and *Home Movies,* the wild world of an eight-year-old and his divorced mom. The Warner Bros. network is pinning its hopes on *Baby Blues,* another cartoon-strip–based series, and *The Downtowners,* built around four wacky roommates in the big city.

INTERVIEW: A COMIC STRIP
AND COMIC BOOK ARTIST

I wanted to be a cartoonist ever since I was about six years old. I remember drawing posters for school plays and was known as "the kid who could draw" in my school in suburban South Bend. I also frequently drew letters and posters for the Cub Scouts and other things like that. I wasn't an athlete, that's for sure, but excelled in drawing, which made me popular to a certain extent.

I went to school at Notre Dame, and toward the end of my college years, I began picking up some freelance work around town. I did a series of educational slides for a community hospital, and one summer I traveled around to various art fairs doing caricatures. I have pretty much stopped this except for some cartooning and caricatures that I still do for private parties—bar mitzvahs and the like.

After finishing school, I traveled for about a year and a half, and when I returned, I set up my studio to do freelance cartooning. I put together a portfolio of some of my better work done in college and took it around to the local paper. I impressed the woman in the art department in charge of commissioning illustrations from freelancers, as well as the editorial department editor, who told me that they published cartoons on local issues by local artists. So I studied the paper to familiarize myself with some of the local issues, drew a few cartoons, and brought them over to the paper. They bought several and that was the start of a three-year relationship in which, at the height of it, I was doing four political cartoons a week, as well as illustration.

Later, when I got to Chicago, I did illustrations for the feature section of the *Tribune,* but my contact there suddenly decided to leave and I was without any further assignments. That is one of the hazards that you run into in this business. You meet someone who likes your work, and one day your services are no longer needed when the successor takes over. I have been freelancing since arriving in Chicago for about ten years now, with one exception. For a two-year stint, I put in about twenty-four hours a week with a publication called *In These Times,* which is now published biweekly. In addition to this work, I was shooting stats and handling assignments in the art department for illustrations and political cartoons.

About five years ago they computerized the paper, so they no longer needed stats, and I was laid off. I still do illustrations for them on a freelance basis, and these are fairly regular assignments. When I was working full time, they paid me $70 per week for one or two illustrations. It was nothing sensational, but it was steady money. I am still on their payroll, but it's all freelance work now.

What it amounts to is this: there are those who draw in a cartoon style, but all they are really doing is illustrating. The way I see it, cartooning is both writing and drawing—if you do not write anything to go with your drawings, then you are an illustrator, not a cartoonist. Don't get me wrong, I'm not knocking that. I draw a lot of illustrations right now, but if that's all you do, I just don't think you are a cartoonist. There are probably at least a couple hundred of what I would call cartoonists working in the Chicago area, and there's a huge animation industry as well.

I prefer to stick to comic books even though I started in political cartooning. I must admit that my branch of the comic books is a little strange. It doesn't pay very well, but it does offer a lot of creative freedom. If you can draw mainstream comics for comic book publishers you can do fairly well. So do those who do cartoon strips for newspapers, almost all of which are syndicated and appear in hundreds of papers across the country. These syndicates pay beginners about $20,000 a year, but you can be dropped just like that if the strip does not attract enough readers.

Creating comic books is a whole different ball game. Those who work the big, well-known books—such as *Batman* and *Superman*—can make up to $60,000 a year. But my stuff is not mainstream. You might have called it "underground" twenty-five years ago, but today it is considered alternative. Alternative comic books are relatively unstable commodities. Right now, those who are doing them successfully can earn upward of the mid-$50s off their comic books alone. Frankly, while I would like to work mainstream and make more money, I like the freedom of expression that I now enjoy and can probably make more money in this area if I work at it.

But the real money is to be made by selling your concepts to the movies or to TV. Here you can be talking about a sizable chunk of money—$100,000 and more. The smallest advance is $25,000, and that's the very least you can make if you hit on TV or film, but there are catches. They may want the rights to the character that you have conceived, which you may not want to give up since you can make a lot of money marketing the same strip to secondary publications. So you can make a lot of money, but you can also lose by giving up your character rights.

A benefit of working in this field is that cartooning is basically an express or postal type of business. Most cartoonists do not live anywhere near the publishers. If you have the talent and create a character that is different or distinctive, you can live just about anywhere and still make a good living. There is hardly ever any need to travel any distance. I've worked for years with people both in the Chicago area and far removed from it. For example, I'm changing my publishers soon because I was offered more with my new publisher. I'll be doing some scriptwriting for Marvel Comics, and I've just completed a big job for another outfit. There's some risk in dealing with newly formed companies, but most of those that are established are pretty good about payment.

I also do a lot of illustration work, and here I don't have to worry about rejection, because most of the assignments I get are from people who know me and my style. They give me jobs because they have confidence in me and like my work. I send my current publisher all projects that I complete and seldom, if ever, do they reject anything. When I do an illustration, they first approve a rough sketch, because they are usually commissioning me to do a piece for a specific article. If I do a piece for a big slick magazine, they ask for ideas and may or may not buy it. Generally, I don't work on such a basis, but sometimes, it's worth the risk.

For me, the worst part of cartooning is the conflict between what I want to do artistically and what will make me the most money. As a result, I have gone down some paths that, in the short run, have not paid so well. To be frank, had I really wanted to do political cartooning, I would probably be in a more secure position than I am now. It's a good job, if you are lucky enough to get one, and I was with a fairly good-size paper and had friends in the industry who were willing to help me. I lost my job in political cartooning because of a change in the company authority. That wasn't what soured me on the business of creating political cartoons, however. I simply found it boring to do that type of work each day, and I didn't like how conservative some of my coworkers were. I enjoy writing my own stories and working with characters that I've created, and I didn't have the freedom to do this with this particular paper. I find that any work I do has to challenge and intrigue me. I've turned down work that I didn't believe I could handle or do well. Once, I was asked to do a realistic drawing of the president, and I felt that this was not something that I could do well. Ordinarily, though, I don't turn down work because I may not be in agreement with the person's politics or philosophy.

My typical day varies, but ordinarily I am up by 6:30 A.M. and am at my drawing board at about 8:45 A.M. after I have showered, read the paper, and had some coffee. I try to use the hours between nine and eleven for anything that I have to write, but if I have something to draw, I usually start around eleven and work until about one, when I have lunch. Then it's back to the drawing board, and I work until about six o'clock. If I have a lot of work, I may put in another hour or two after dinner, but I try to avoid this. It's simply too many hours to work in one day. But there are many days when I have to take care of errands, and I don't begin to work until the afternoon.

If you are not forced to put in this kind of work and don't find drawing especially to your liking, then this is not the career for you. It's more than just disciplining yourself; it's a compulsion. It's something that you can't help and that becomes pretty much an obsession. Yeah, sometimes it becomes a grind and I hate it and I find myself getting backaches and my hands getting stiff. It can definitely drain a lot of energy and it can be very hard physically, and if you're neurotic, you can find yourself questioning your work or your ability. So the work has its ups and downs, but as I said, it's an obsession, and I'd probably get bored to death or sick if I had to do something else.

There are times when it's beautiful out and I find that I'd like to be at the beach or sailing or something like that, but if you are on a deadline, you have to resist those urges to do something else or to take a break. As I've said before, you've got to have this compulsion to do cartooning. If you don't have it, I doubt very much that you'll make it successfully as a cartoonist. Personal problems can interfere with the work, but if you are disciplined, you should be able to surmount any problems that may come up.

You could say that in cartooning, the world is your oyster. Everything becomes fodder for your work. You may not be so hot in drawing, but you have to write well. In fact, I think you could say that drawing too well could be a liability. There are too many cartoonists who can make beautiful drawings, but don't have much to say. Everybody tends to imitate the style of those who succeed. My drawing is just so-so. I am by no means a great artist. So again, I say that if you want to succeed in this business, you've got to know about a lot of stuff—you've got to read, go to the movies, watch TV, and develop interests in and a natural curiosity for what's going on around you and all over the world.

For the future, the news is good and bad. The real growth area in cartooning is in the field of animation and TV. But the problem is that these areas are not ordinarily a means of expressing yourself as an individual—responsible for the whole ball of wax. Instead, you are part of a team, and to me the real crux of cartooning is that in cartooning you are the creator, the one who writes and draws everything. There have never been a lot of cartoonists, and, to a certain extent, some of the already small markets that create or publish cartoons have shrunk. Magazines, for instance, used to publish a lot of gag cartoons. Now that market has almost disappeared, although in recent years it is showing signs of making a comeback. Comic books, however, have been a growth industry as more and more books are starting out every year and succeeding. Many films have even been based on comic book stories. The future of cartoon strips is debatable. To a great degree, it has become tougher to make it as a strip cartoonist because the number of newspapers has shrunk to extremely low levels over the past few decades. This has also adversely affected political cartooning. In addition, political cartooning is a very conservative field—more so than any other area of cartooning. So unless you do a particular kind of strip, it's hard to make it in this field. Free weekly newspapers like the *Reader* and *New City* in Chicago have been using more and more cartoonists, but there are drawbacks here too. For one, the pay is not so hot, and if you want to be syndicated, you almost have to do this yourself. On top of that, it takes a long time to get enough clients, even if you are doing the syndication yourself. Political, or editorial, cartooning is even tougher. It's very competitive. If you can land a job on a major newspaper, it can be a good job with a good salary and benefits. And if you should win a Pulitzer, your problems are over and your job is secure.

CHAPTER 2

THE HISTORY OF CARTOONS—FROM *B.C.* TO *A BUG'S LIFE*

You might say that cartooning is as old as the hills, or, perhaps more properly put, as old as the caves. Many archaeologists believe that cartooning goes back to antiquity—to the caricatures and primitive drawings found on ancient Egyptian walls and Greek vases. As originally defined, cartoons were preliminary sketches for serious paintings or architectural drawings. It was not until the midnineteenth century that cartoons began to humorously satirize subjects for the amusement of readers.

ENGLISH ORIGINS

The origin of the cartoon as a satirical drawing poking fun at some individual, topic, or place can be traced to an Englishman named William Hogarth (1697–1764). He had all that it takes to be a fine artist, but his disgust at the predominantly low morals of members of polite society drove him to take a moral stance focusing on seamy and contemporary themes. Thus Hogarth abandoned the traditional viewpoint of creating art for the sake of posterity in order to rail against the evils of his time. He lashed out at his contemporaries more and more often through his satirical engravings. Starting in 1732, he produced several series of engravings—*The Rake's Progress, Marriage à la Mode, The Harlot's Progress*—that were fiercely realistic. Indeed, their very realism made them unfit for the upper strata of the arts, considered the arena of mythology, gentle scenes, and portraits. But Hogarth's realism had a great impact on the people, and suddenly there was a new kind of art in which technique and emotions were bent to comment on social and moral issues.

Hogarth inspired other early notables in cartooning, primarily Thomas Rowlandson and George Cruikshank. Rowlandson (1756–1827) was England's first great "cartoonist." He started as a part-time caricaturist but because of heavy gambling debts soon turned to drawing full time. Working primarily in copperplate etchings, Rowlandson's complicated, somewhat rowdy sketches poked fun at all levels of society, but he reserved his sharpest barbs for the rich and powerful. Due to the development of technology in journalism and the increase in newspaper distribution, he was able to reach a vastly wider audience than Hogarth. Rowlandson's work could be regarded as a forerunner of modern cartooning, since one series, *Tour of Dr. Syntax,* used the same method of storytelling or continuity employed by some comic strips of today.

George Cruikshank (1792–1878), also English, was born when Rowlandson was thirty-six and already making a name for himself as a social commentator. Largely self-taught, Cruikshank was creative, irrepressible, and possessed a sharp sense of man's inhumanity to man. His etchings mostly satirized the rich and powerful—industrialists, landowners, and corrupt politicians. Although believed by many to be a lesser artist than his predecessors, he was able to reach a still greater audience as the numbers of newspapers and those who were literate continued to increase. The modern meaning of the word *cartoon* dates back to when Cruikshank was about fifty. In the minds of many observers, he was the link between classical satire and the modern cartoon.

The evils that accompanied the industrialization of England, including pollution, child labor abuses, and various abuses of the working classes, became an endless source of inspiration for Hogarth, Rowlandson, and Cruikshank. This resulted in an almost unbroken stream of social satire that lasted over a period of almost 200 years. Many artists in England and other European countries protested the moral decadence of the wealthy classes and the wretched conditions of the poorer classes. Nowhere was this done more vividly and with more impact than in the work of the great Spanish painter and satirist Francisco Goya (1746–1828). His *Caprichios,* published in 1799, was a powerful rendering of the human condition, and his savage imagery played a prominent role in the development of the nineteenth-century European cartoon as an instrument of protest.

The cartoon as an instrument of humor can be traced back to Frenchman Charles Philipon, who can be considered the father of the modern humor magazine. His magazine, *La Charivari,* launched in 1832, became the pinnacle of humor magazines, and cartoonists of distinction clamored to be included in its pages. One cartoonist featured in the magazine was Honoré Daumier (1808–79), perhaps the greatest of all French cartoonists, whose lithographs deftly satirized midnineteenth-century France. Largely because of the success of *La Charivari,* the British humor magazine *Punch* was founded in 1841 by Henry Mayhew, who modeled its pages after the social criticism of Philipon. It soon carved out its own niche and included in its ranks the talented cartoonists John Leech, who lampooned British politics, and Richard Doyle, who created the magazine's famous cover. Later, other talented artists, including John Tenniel, Charles Keene, and, especially, the model *Punch* cartoonist George Du Maurier (1834–96), were added to its ranks. Throughout the nineteenth century, *Punch* maintained its lofty position as the leading humor magazine in Britain despite the rise and fall of numerous other humor journals, including *Vanity Fair.*

CARTOONING IN AMERICA

Prior to the Civil War, American cartooning was based largely on the English and European tradition of caricature and political lampooning. In Colonial America, within the restrictions of the Alien and Sedition Acts, England and the Parliament were attacked by many cartoonists, chief among them Benjamin Franklin. Franklin was most famous for his drawing of a bisected snake, each segment of which was labeled with the names of the various colonies, and which carried the legend "Join or Die." Although the cartoon industry's growth was spurred by the development of commercial lithography and the 1829 election of Andrew Jackson, who was often attacked by cartoonists, cartooning had little impact before the outbreak of the Civil War in 1861. That year's election of Abraham Lincoln, tall, homespun, and bearded, inspired many of the most savage cartoons of the period.

Following the Civil War, an Englishman, Frank Leslie, published a series of comic magazines carrying the work of William Newman, formerly a leading artist of *Punch.* Of the cartoonists of the period, none were more famous than Thomas Nast (see "Editorial or Political Cartoons" in Chapter 1) and Walt McDougall. McDougall's most famous cartoon, popularly known as *Belshazzar's Feast,* is believed to have tipped the 1884 presidential election to Grover Cleveland.

From 1900 to 1920, Pulitzer prize–winning cartoonist John T. McCutcheon, beloved for his drawings of Hoosier youngsters in the summertime, dominated. He covered both the Spanish-American War and the Boer War for the *Chicago Tribune* and won the Pulitzer prize in 1932 for his grim comments on the Depression. A new generation of cartoonists followed, many of them producing political cartoons that were irreverent and angry, including Pulitzer prize winners Rollin Kirby, Jay Norwood "Ding" Darling, Nelson Harding, and Dan Fitzpatrick. Following a brief hiatus during World War I, cartoonists Kirby and Fitzpatrick again came into their own, producing cartoons that were biting and funny. Other great cartoonists of the postwar period included Vaughn Shoemaker of the *Chicago Daily News* and Jacob Burck of the *Chicago Times,* both Pulitzer prize winners.

Following World War II, Herbert L. Block (Herblock) dominated the field, winning three Pultizers, in 1942, 1954, and 1979, while displaying a magnificent hatred of pomposity and fakery. For a time, Bill Mauldin, whose bitter yet often funny war cartoons featured GIs who were disillusioned and grim, ran away with cartooning honors. He took the Pulitzer in 1945 and 1959.

Panel or gag cartoons came into vogue in America during the 1840s, with the innovation of lithography. This new technique enhanced the transfer of illustrations directly from stones to paper. This was much simpler and less expensive than copperplates and engravings. Starting with the *Old American Comic Almanac* of 1841, dozens of comic almanacs featuring single-panel cartoons of satirical and often low, but not pornographic, nature were regularly published.

The 1870s saw the rise of the first generation of truly funny American cartoonists, whose work appeared in such widely circulated humor magazines as *Puck* and *Judge.* Many of these artists did Sunday comic pages in the 1890s, but all were primarily panel cartoonists. Included in their number were A. B. Frost, Kemble, C. J. Taylor, Charles Dana Gibson, and Thomas S. Sullivant.

The start of the twentieth century marked a turn toward sharper wit among a new generation of cartoonists. Leaders of this group included Carl Anderson (later famous for *Henry*), George Herriman (*Fritz the Cat*), and Robert F. Outcault, creator of *Hogan's Alley,* which originated in Joseph Pulitzer's New York *World.* This immensely popular strip featured the Yellow Kid and dealt with life in the tenements of that period. By the early twenties a new kind of disillusionment set in, as seen in cartoons featured in magazines like *Vanity Fair* and the *New Yorker,* which used the cynical gag cartoon as one of the primary tools in its armory. Since its founding in 1925, the *New Yorker* has published an estimated one thousand cartoons. Its list of contributors is almost a Who's Who in the panel cartooning world and includes John Held Jr., Helen Hokinson, Gluyas Williams, Peter Arno, Otto Soglow, and above all James Thurber. This impressive stable of cartoonists took potshots at civic pride, boosterism, social pretension, and smugness. Their efforts were continued by other great names in cartooning, including William Steig, Charles Addams, Sam Cobean, George Price, and Saul Steinberg.

Indirectly, the *New Yorker*'s overwhelming success with gag cartoons spurred more widely circulated magazines such as *Collier's,* the *Saturday Evening Post, Woman's*

Day, and many others to get on board, and they too began to feature panel cartoons. By the 1950s, there was scarcely a periodical in the land that did not carry some kind of panel cartoon. The *Saturday Evening Post,* for example, was rumored to run about thirty cartoons a week out of about four thousand submitted. The daily newspapers, which received most of their cartoon strips from syndicates, began to scatter single-panel or gag cartoons throughout the paper to give readers some lighter moments while browsing the classifieds or other sections. Some cartoons, like George Clark's *Neighbors* and William G. Clark's *Side Glances,* featured middle-class comedy. Others, such as those of Lichty and Reamer Keller, poked fun at just about everything. Famous cartoonists of the period included J. R. Williams, creator of *Out Our Way,* which tells the story of a small middle-class town in America; Gluyas Williams, known primarily for his *New Yorker* panels that dissected the suburban upper-middle classes; and Fontaine Fox, creator of *Toonerville Folks* and its off-the-tracks trolley, whose talents with perspective and off-kilter horizons, poles, people, and vehicles made him famous and beloved. Fox's cartoon strip, the third oldest daily cartoon in the country, ran for more than forty years.

In the 1950s and '60s, panel cartoons grew increasingly popular and saw artists Jules Feiffer, David Levine, and Edward Sorel lampooning national fads and trends, politicians, suburban life, sex, nudity, and many other facets of our society. The most popular series at this time were those using gentle humor to comment on domestic situations. Ted Key's *Hazel,* about a sarcastic and critical maid who is the de facto head of the household she is supposed to serve, and the innocent *Family Circus,* which tells the story of an average American home based on cartoonist Bill Keane's own home life, are just two popular examples. Bill Hoest's *The Lockhorns* portrayed a bickering, petty American married couple with lighthearted humor.

Inevitably, cartoonists began to specialize and today many devote their work to a single issue or interest such as medicine, fashion, the financial world, or the courts. Sports cartoons were popular for years to depict real-life sporting events, but sports photography gradually usurped their place in the papers. A few practitioners, such as Bill Gallo of the *New York Daily News,* still produce these niche cartoons.

As our society changes, so do the cartoons and comic strips created to reflect and comment on social themes and interests. While vestiges of popular old-style cartoons still remain in the Sunday pages, another kind of cartoon characterized by sarcasm, with pitiless plots and without illusion about the human race, has emerged, as represented by Gary Larson's *The Far Side,* Dan Piraro's *Bizzaro,* and the work of Gahan Wilson and Ed Gorey. At the forefront of the new American cartoonists are Jim Borgman, Steve Benson, Tom Toles, and Signe Wilkinson, who happens to be one of an increasing number of women cartoonists who have come into their own in recent years.

CARTOONS THAT MOVE—ANIMATION

As far back as the seventeenth century, when the Chinese attempted to give motion to images via the shadow play, man has attempted to animate images. In the nineteenth century, the Frenchman Peter Mark Roget demonstrated the phenomenon known as "persistence of image," in which a given image remains fixed in a person's mind for a fraction of a second after the eye has ceased seeing it. Thus, if you take a series of images, each image minutely different from the previous one, and view them in rapid succession, you get the impression of motion. This optical illusion is the basis of the animated cartoon, as well as the principal used to create motion pictures.

Zoetropes and Rotoscopes

In the 1830s, W. G. Horner, a British watchmaker, invented what was probably the first practical demonstration of animation—the Zoetrope, a drum containing a series of hand-drawn images in sequence. As the drum revolved, the images appeared to move. Emile Reynaud, a French inventor, went one step further with the praxinoscope, the first projector used to show moving images. It was the invention of the film camera, however, that made animation feasible. In 1906, a newspaper cartoonist and filmmaker, J. S. Blackton, made the first cartoon film, *Humorous Phases of Funny Faces,* which had as its premise one turn of the camera crank, one picture. In this way, the animated cartoon was permanently tied to the movie camera. In 1911, cartoonist Windsor McCay worked with Blackton to produce an animated version of his popular newspaper cartoon *Little Nemo*. However, it was McCay's *Gertie the Dinosaur* that really established animation as an art form. Fascinated viewers saw Gertie dancing on the screen, balancing a ball on her nose, and pulling up trees.

Meanwhile, many early animators were seeking ways to make the new cartoon art profitable. First they had to overcome the primary obstacle—the enormous amount of work involved in producing only a few minutes of film animation. A number of technical processes were devised to accomplish just this. J. R. Bray and Earl Hurd developed the process for drawing on celluloid, the so-called cel process (described in Chapter 3, "A Look at the Work"). Raul Barre designed the peg system, which allowed for the correct positioning of animated drawings in front of the camera through the use of pegs. Max Fleischer, who went on to fame as the talented producer of United Productions of America (UPA) cartoons in the 1920s, invented a device known as the rotoscope, which was used in tracing live action as animated footage. The first animation studio was established by Bray and Barre in 1915. It featured an impressive list of cartoon stars that were mostly borrowed from the newspaper comics, such as the Katzenjammer Kids, Krazy Kat, and Mutt and Jeff. A few popular characters, however, were developed by studio artists. Perhaps the most popular cartoon character of the silent film era was Felix the Cat, created by Pat Sullivan in 1917 and perfected by Otto Mesmer in the 1920s.

The Disney Revolution

It was during this period that the legendary Walt Disney entered the scene and rented a small studio in Hollywood, with his brother Roy as his manager and chief financial backer. Disney sent for Ub Iwerks and several other associates who had worked with him in a short-lived venture producing animated commercials in Kansas City in 1919. Disney proceeded to create a series of successful shorts. The first, called *Alice in Cartoonland,* featured live action and animation. Next, collaborating with several associates, Disney produced a series entitled *Oswald, the Lucky Rabbit,* which though very well received was dropped when creditors threatened to take several characters away from Disney— he had relinquished the rights to them, a mistake he never repeated. Undaunted, Disney promptly thought up a new character, Mickey Mouse. His first two Mickey Mouse cartoons were silent, but the third, *Steamboat Willie,* had sound and became an instant hit in 1928. With *Steamboat Willie,* Disney's reputation was firmly established. (Interestingly, Walt Disney did all the voices in the Mickey Mouse films, starting with *Steamboat Willie* in 1928 to *Fun and Fancy Free* in 1946.) Never one to rest on his laurels, Disney soon produced another series, the *Silly Symphonies,* to accompany the Mickey Mouse series. With a different cast of characters in each film, the *Silly Symphonies* enabled Disney's animators to experiment with stories that relied less on gags and sly humor and more on mood and emotion. Eventually, the *Silly Symphonies* became a training ground for all Disney artists as they prepared for the advent of full-length animated feature films.

In 1934, Disney informed his animators that he wanted to make an animated feature film to be known as *Snow White and the Seven Dwarves*. While some were skeptical at first, eventually everyone was caught up in Disney's enthusiasm, and the work began. The film took three years to complete, but no one could have predicted what a spectacular hit it would become when it was released in 1937. It was the highest grossing film of all time until the release of *Gone with the Wind* in 1939. Other full-length animated features, like *Pinocchio* and *Fantasia* in 1940, *Dumbo* in 1941, *Bambi* in 1942, and *Lady and the Tramp* in 1955 further enhanced Disney's reputation as a master producer of animated films. Soon every other animation studio was imitating Disney with the exception of Max Fleischer's, which wisely gave cartoon hits Betty Boop and Popeye human characteristics rather than animal features.

Disney's main competition during this period came from Warner Bros. Studios, founded by former Disney animators Hugh Harman, Rudolph Ising, and Isadore "Friz" Freleng. The studio began by trying to imitate Disney's success with animals. But by the mid-1930s, Warner Bros. developed its own distinctive, fresh brand of humor, which remains funny today. Also, rather than compete directly with Disney in the field of full-length feature animation, it concentrated on the animated short. In 1930, Harman, Ising, and Freleng created their immensely successful Looney Tunes series. When they eventually left, the studio parlayed the talents of other outstanding animators—Chuck Jones, Tex Avery, and Bobe Cannon—into a string of immortal animated cartoon characters including Daffy Duck, Bugs Bunny, Porky Pig, the Road Runner, Wile E. Coyote, Tweety, Sylvester, and many more.

In 1940, MGM made its mark on the animation scene by launching the *Tom and Jerry* series. This wildly popular animated cartoon was the creation of two young and talented studio animators, William Hanna and Joseph Barbera. Barbera wrote the stories, made the sketches, and came up with the gags, while Hanna provided the direction. They went on to win five Pulitzer prizes with this hugely successful series. A few years later, in 1944, Gene Kelly realized his longtime dream of dancing with a cartoon character by teaming with Hanna and Barbera to produce the impressive *Anchors Aweigh.* Following the close of MGM's animation studio in 1957, Hanna and Barbera produced a series of popular features for television: *The Flintstones, Huckleberry Hound, Ruff and Ready,* and *Quick Draw McGraw.* Hanna-Barbera rescued the floundering animation field by offering more jobs for artists, writers, and technicians than any other studio since Disney in the 1930s.

Following a dormant period during World War II, the new UPA captured audiences with the fresh and slightly off-kilter characters Mr. Magoo and Gerald McBoing Boing. But a slump in the industry eventually led to several studios closing their doors. Thus the successes of Ralph Bakshi were all the more spectacular. One of his greatest animated films was the smash success *Lord of the Rings* (1978).

After a prolonged slump in the 1970s, the animation industry rebounded. Nowhere was the trend more obvious than with the Disney Company. Disney launched an ambitious production schedule of feature-length cartoons based on its stock in trade, the musical fairy tale. Its efforts paid off with the success of the *Little Mermaid* (1989), *Beauty and the Beast* (1991), and *The Lion King* (1994). The only Disney creation during this period that did not draw large audiences or big grosses at the box office was *The Hunchback of Notre Dame,* and it was by no means a failure. Other studios tried to challenge Disney, with some success. Perhaps the most successful was that of former Disney animator Don Bluth. Bluth's releases included *The Secret of NIMH* (1982), *An American Tale* (1986), and *The Land Before Time* (1988). Independently produced features included *Fern Gully* and *The Last Rain Forest* (1992).

On television, most animated shows are aimed at children and do not garner attention from the public and the critics. One very notable exception is *The Simpsons.* Introduced on Fox TV in 1992, *The Simpsons* is slanted toward adults, with adult themes and humor. Several other prime-time animated television shows, including *King of the Hill* and *Beavis and Butthead,* are now being shown in reruns—a sure sign of their success. There are many new shows in production by major television networks hoping to bank on the success of these animated situation comedies.

COMPUTER ANIMATION

Disney experimented with computers in 1982 with the release of *Tron,* with mixed results. In the mid-1990s, the Disney Company, in association with a computer software company, Pixar, introduced computer animation. This mixture of traditional cartoon graphics with computer graphics, called *computer-assisted imagery*—as opposed to computer-generated imagery—employs the computer at every stage of the process. First, hand-drawn storyboard sketches outline the film's general plot or story. Next, an animator duplicates the sketches through a computer model. This is known as a *wire mesh* because it is based on a fine network of lines. Finally, other animators fill in the outlines and add texture, background, lighting, color, scenes, and visual effects, also called *pat-ons.* The melding together of the different scenes into a cohesive film is then plotted on the computer. This total animation process, hand-drawn and then plotted by computer, was used to create the feature *Toy Story* (1995), in which the toys moved with computer-generated precision yet enjoyed the freedom of hand-drawn characters.

The creation of just a few minutes of film using traditional cel-generated animation would employ too many artists and require too many working hours to make a full-length feature film practical. Thus computers, alone or in combination with cel-generated animation, are used with increasing frequency in all stages of the production process to create various visual effects, characters, backgrounds, and even to serve as the camera in filming animated characters. The role of the computer in the production process will be examined in greater detail in Chapter 3, "A Look at the Work."

INTERVIEW: A SENIOR ANIMATOR

I work for an outfit called Will Vinton Studios in Portland, Oregon, where I am a senior animator hired to work in the computer department doing computer as well as other kinds of animation. Our main business is production of short television commercials. We do the M&M's commercials that you hopefully have seen on TV. We also do commercials for some foreign countries, including England, France, and Germany. We've just gone through a hiring period at our studio and we have over three hundred workers.

I've been with Vinton since '96. When I finished school at Columbia College in Chicago, where I received my B.A. in film and video in 1986, I worked in various production studios in Chicago. Through a friend of mine, Vinton saw my reel, which had many of the commercials that I had worked on while I was in Chicago. They hired me because they felt that I could be trained to use "Lightwave," which is a computer program that we use. They were willing to give me some time to become accustomed to working on computers. It was about a year before I became familiar enough to use a computer to do animation. As a beginner, I used whatever animation skills I had or could learn to do computer animation. I started animating a couple of shots and slowly I got a little better and a little faster. After about a year or two I felt more like I knew what I was doing and was comfortable doing it.

In most of the M&M's spots that we do, we build a character in the computer and then manipulate him in the computer. However, I'm working on a project now for Glade in which I take drawings, make them look like a kid drew them, and then interject them into a live-action scene. We're using the computer as a big camera and a compositing device, which saves us having to figure out all of the camera moves and animation moves.

I'd say that any place that has the up-to-date equipment that you will need is a pretty good bet for a job. It's possible to do computer animation anywhere in the country if they have the right equipment. On the West coast, there are many studios. They've got a little more pull perhaps because the advertisers in Chicago and New York are used to coming out here to make a project happen. They know the studios and their abilities. Agencies out East give us ideas to put into animation. I've worked at the Leo Burnett Advertising

Agency, which is headquartered in Chicago. Other studios in Chicago, such as Calabash, know what they are doing but may not have the pull or influence of the studios on the West coast. We're perhaps the main studio in Portland for doing 3-D animation with stop motion or computers. We don't do much cell animation, but I am hoping to change that. We can handle a job with some cell animation, but we are not really set up to do any major productions in cell animation.

If you have the proper tools you can always get a job with one of the bigger studios such as Disney, Universal, or Pixar. They have hundreds of talented animators at their disposal so they can pick and choose whom they hire. You can try to get in there, but it's hard. If your portfolio does not show the talents they are looking for, they will tell you that. They do hire beginners. Unfortunately, most of their new hires are from Cal Arts [California Institute of the Arts]. A Cal Arts résumé is like the Cadillac of the animation business. Disney and some of the larger animation studios recruit a lot of people out of Cal Arts because it trains everyone in Disney's style of animation. Also Disney has invested money in that school and looks there first.

Computer animation is mostly a growth industry. But I've noticed that many recent projects are not that good. I did think that *Tarzan* was really good. Everyone seems to be working on stories like *Tarzan* that they believe will be popular with the public. Two other good examples of this trend are *A Bug's Life* and *Antz*. I liked *A Bug's Life* better because they covered all sorts of bugs and you got a sense of watching an entirely new world, and it was funny and exciting at the same time. Both of these features had a lot of traditional drawing of characters on paper and trying to get the right look of the character, and they then transferred all of this into the computer.

Job security is pretty good. Many of the studios today hire people on a project by project basis. You could work on a feature for two years, and when the feature's over, they may fire you or lay you off. Then you have to start out again and look for more work. I'd rather work for two years on something that people know about than on something that will never be seen. Many of these short-term projects exist.

I can't really say what animators are earning out here, but I know at Vinton we have people who check to see what the going rates for salaries are in comparable studios. We can adjust our salary scale up or down depending upon what they find to be the going rate.

Hours can be very hectic in this business. I know people in L.A. who push fourteen-hour days and sometimes weekends. Many studios in L.A. and other places on the West Coast are unionized. This guarantees that you will work for a definite period of time and that you are paid at the right rate. We don't have a union at Vinton, but we do have 401-G retirement programs for employees. It is not like other places where I worked for two weeks or a month and was let go and had to find other employment.

My advice to all beginning cartoonists is to start assembling a portfolio or reel of your best work. Whatever you do, don't send them the original. Send them a copy, which is all they will require to judge your qualifications.

INTERVIEW: A PROFESSOR AND FORMER DISNEY PRODUCER AND DIRECTOR

I worked for Disney Studios for eighteen years as a producer-director and am currently teaching several courses here at Columbia in film production, editing, and animation. I produced a picture called *Pete's Dragon,* which is a combination of live action and animation, at Disney. Many years ago, when I was an actor, I did voices for several Disney features, but I was not an animator per se. I am currently teaching a course at Columbia called "Animation 2," which is about storyboarding for animation. I also taught a course in "Animation Production Studios" in the past.

Besides the big studios—Disney, Hanna-Barbera, and Universal—that produce feature films today, many other studios produce commercials for TV. One of the major studios, Fox, also has a unit that makes commercials for TV. Don Bluth and Jerry Goldman have done several features for Fox, including the *Mouse's Tale.* When I was with Disney for eight years, I knew most of the animators. Bluth and Goldman worked on *Anastasia* and some other features, and they worked with me in the production of *Pete's Dragon.*

Even with the increased use of the computer in animation today, you still have to have the drawing and the storyboarding skills. You need to know things like composition and light. But the computer has greatly impacted the industry. *Toy Story,* for instance, was done entirely by computer. Even the little boy and his mother, the main live characters, were created by the computer. Another big use of the computer is in stop-motion animation. Using a computer makes the camera work much simpler. We give beginning animators a year or so to learn drawing and traditional computer skills and another year or so for learning individual programs.

Not everybody has to have the same kinds of drawing skills that would be necessary to get a job at Disney. If you look at a lot of the cartoon shows on TV on Saturday mornings, they have a different kind of animation. A lot of animation is done for videogames. It's a simpler kind of animation at this point, but it's a growing field. The demand is for good, creative people who are able to work well with other people.

It's certainly a collaborative enterprise to produce animated films. Hundreds of people are involved in producing animated features. Different people write the script, compose and score the music, handle sound effects, and more. For example, layout people work closely with the director of the film. They take the storyboards and actually compose the shots and backgrounds that will be used for animation. They don't necessarily create the backgrounds or the characters. Other people do that.

Animators are in demand right now, but the market is like any other. As more and more people get into the field, the competition becomes fiercer. Animation is part of show business, which can be very erratic. It still takes exceptional talent and self-motivation to do well.

CHAPTER 3

A LOOK AT THE WORK

As discussed in Chapter 1, cartooning manifests itself in many ways. Cartoons may be simple panel or gag drawings for magazines, cartoon strips for newspapers, running features for comic books, illustrations for greeting cards and children's books, or artwork commissioned by advertising agencies. Cartooning is also used in what is undoubtedly the fastest growing part of the industry—animation. Once you have polished your cartooning skills, you have many diverse and exciting avenues to explore in finding the career that's right for you.

CARTOONING FOR MAGAZINES

Magazine or gag cartoons are unique in that they are able to stand on their own. You are not locked into any single character or stock of characters, as you would be in a cartoon strip or comic book, so you are freed to explore a range of topics with many different characters. Another benefit of magazine cartooning is that it can be a springboard to other branches of the industry, including comic strips, children's books, greeting cards, and calendars, and to working with other media.

Magazines are a great avenue for beginning cartoonists because most magazines publish quite a few cartoons each month and pay up to $500 for a single cartoon. Also, many cartoonists find magazines more receptive to the work of beginners than newspapers and other venues. Though the magazine market—like every other market for cartooning and animation—is dominated by established artists, it is still the easiest place to get your work published. General interest or large consumer magazines, however, are the toughest markets for a beginning cartoonist to break into. They also tend to pay higher fees for the cartoons they commission. But they do consider the work of beginners, and if your work is fresh and distinctive (see Chapter 4) you have as good a chance as anyone of seeing your work published.

Many special-interest magazines buy cartoons for publication each month and often pay almost as well as the consumer magazines. These include medical publications, trade journals (for the construction, health, retail, fashion, and real estate fields, among many others), men's magazines, religious magazines, sports magazines, magazines for children and teenagers, pet magazines, and many others. Editors of these publications know that their readers love to laugh, so they are always on the lookout for the work of skilled cartoonists. On-line magazines are also becoming a viable market for all types of cartoons.

CREATING AND SUBMITTING CARTOONS

For magazine cartooning as for all branches of the field, you've got to have drawing and writing talent, flexibility and adaptability, persistence, and perhaps most important of all, a deep and abiding love of cartooning in order to succeed. These skills will help you get noticed in this competitive field and will also arm you for dealing with the rejection you will face while getting established. With that in mind, here are a few tips for producing and marketing cartoons for magazines.

• Jot down some ideas. Put down as many as you can and then focus on the strongest. Be sure to create panels similar in format to the cartoons you see in most magazines. Don't try to submit comic strip gags to magazines; this is not their typical format.

• Pencil in your cartoon on heavyweight typing paper. Don't start inking until you feel that you have the cartoon just right. Go over your pencil sketch with black India ink or a felt-tip marker. Be sure that the lines are bold enough to reproduce well even if the cartoon is printed very small.

• Learn to work quickly. You can hardly expect to make a decent salary if it takes you a week to draw one cartoon. Because the rejection rate on cartoons is so high, at least at the beginning of your career, you need to produce as many as fifteen cartoons a day just to sell a few a week.

• When your ink dries, be sure to erase your pencil lines completely with a soft art eraser. Alternatively, you can use non-photo blue pencil (available in art supply stores), which will not show up in most reproduction work, thus avoiding the necessity of erasing pencil lines.

• If you want to create a gray wash that will add shading to your cartoons, you can use diluted black ink or water-color. You can create the same effect by using the side of a black pencil on the drawing, blending it with tissue, then spraying it with a fixing agent to prevent smudging. Many magazines use color in their cartoons. You can color your work with concentrated watercolor dyes, either applied directly from the bottle or diluted with water to tone them down a bit. Whatever your color choice, watercolor paint or dye, make sure your black outlines are inked with water-proof India ink, since watercolors and many paint dyes tend to smear and can cause your lines to blur or fade. You may prefer to color your cartoons with markers. These can be applied with India ink lines or with felt-tip pen lines without causing your ink to smear. After your ink or paint dries, you can draw patterns on a color with colored pencils.

• Neatly print or type the caption beneath the drawing, not in a word balloon, which is the style for a cartoon strip.

• On the back of the cartoon, print your name, address, phone number, and E-mail address, if you have one. Put a unique code number on the back of each cartoon to help you keep track of cartoons submitted.

• Mail your cartoons in a flat 9-by-12-inch envelope, remembering to include an 8-by-10-inch cardboard to help protect them. It's a good idea to enclose a self-addressed and stamped envelope for the return of the rejected cartoons. Without a reply envelope, many editors will not even look at your work. Each packet of cartoons you submit for consideration should include ten to twenty panels in order to give the editor a complete idea of your range and style. If you send out one packet to one magazine each week, you can plan on creating between five hundred and a thousand cartoons a year.

Think you are up to this challenge? It can take anywhere from three weeks to a few months to hear from an editor, but once the cartoons are returned (assuming they are rejected), pack them up again and send them to the next editor on the list. While you could send groups of cartoons to more than one magazine at a time, until you become more familiar with the market and the quirks of various publications, it is best to submit your work to one at a time.

As to compiling a mailing list of magazines that might use your cartoons, the hard way is to browse through magazine racks at your supermarket or bookstore and copy the name of the editor, publisher, and so forth. A better way is to subscribe to *Gap ReCap* magazine, which in each issue lists names, addresses, editors, and payment rates for dozens of cartoon-buying magazines. Other helpful tools are the *Writer's Market,* an annual publication, and *Artist's &*

Graphic Designer's Market, both published by Writer's Digest Books, 1507 Dana Avenue, Cincinnati, OH 45207. Both of these books can be purchased in a bookstore or online, or borrowed from your local library.

TOOLS OF THE TRADE

More and more often, computers are coming into play in the handling of cartoon art. You should seriously consider having a personal computer in your studio. Not only can you use the computer to create your work, but many publishers prefer that you E-mail your work to them, or, if in color, send it on disk. This saves them the trouble of scanning and preparing original artwork for publication.

A computer with a CD-ROM allows you to put an encyclopedia of thousands of drawings and many other reference materials at your fingertips. Also, full-color printers are increasingly affordable, and can give you color effects impossible to achieve with watercolors or colored pencils. Many cartoonists use computers to print four-color samples of their work for portfolios and other applications. Many cartoonists also use computers to do their lettering for them, thus freeing them from hours of tedious pen work. Several software products on the market enable you to re-create your own personal lettering style, then save it as a computer font in your hard drive. You print out your captions on a laser printer and paste them onto your original artwork.

What other materials and tools will you need in order to create eye-catching cartoons? A fully stocked shelf of reference materials that contain many photos will help you draw any object with greater detail and clarity. For instance, if you need to draw a knight knocking over a horse-mounted opponent with a lance, photos of these items will help keep your drawings accurate. To be sure, as a cartoonist you do not need to draw realistically, but detailed drawings can help your readers grasp your cartoons more easily. You don't want them to mistake your scooter for a motorcycle!

PANEL CARTOON BOOKS

Magazines are not the only market for panel cartoons. Many established magazines that publish cartoons regularly, like the *New Yorker* or *Playboy,* also publish books featuring the cartoons of their leading artists. If you're not one of these lucky artists, it's up to you to contact publishers that specialize in producing these kinds of books.

To increase the chances of having your book proposal accepted, or even considered, you must send the publisher an enticing, well-crafted proposal. Your work should portray some kind of unique character—think of Garfield the cat, or the animals of Gary Larson's *Far Side*—whatever you feel would interest readers. Submit your best cartoons, including a cover letter explaining the theme of the book and why you believe readers will buy it. List any successes that you have had as a cartoonist, including the names of any on-line or print magazines that may have published your work. Don't forget to include a self-addressed, stamped envelope for the return of your proposal if it is rejected.

CALENDARS

Use the same submission procedure when trying to sell a cartoon calendar publisher on your work. Here you will have to prove your ability to work in color through your sample cartoons. Check *Artist's Market, Writer's Market,* and *Humor and Cartoon Markets,* all published by Writer's Digest, for addresses and other information. If you cannot afford to buy these publications, borrow them from a library. A reference librarian can help you locate these books quickly and easily.

COMIC STRIPS IN NEWSPAPERS

Millions of newspaper readers pore over the comics sections of their favorite newspapers religiously, day in and day out, and especially on Sunday. What about your chances for having one of your cartoon strips accepted in this market? Unfortunately, the market has shrunk in recent years, and to compound matters, many papers today pay less for strips than they used to. Many cartoonists feel that before long every newspaper in the land will publish exactly the same cartoon strips. Already, the same few popular comic strips are syndicated in papers all across the United States, with a few exceptions. However, there is always the possibility that your work will be accepted if it is unique and has something new to say.

SUBMITTING STRIPS TO NEWSPAPERS

When submitting your work to newspapers for publication, the key is to create a unique cast of characters with fresh insights into today's society. A prime example of a successful and popular strip is Charles M. Schulz's crew of characters in *Peanuts,* including Linus, the somewhat simple and innocent little boy, Lucy, his bossy and sarcastic sister, the bumbling and not quite with-it Charlie Brown, and above all, Snoopy, the superhuman dog.

Study the cartoon strips you enjoy reading and analyze just what it is that you like about them. Study the dialog, the content and theme, the style of drawing, and the characters. Then write several comic strip gags. They should be concise and easy to grasp. Try to come up with some strips that are true to your own personality and life experiences. You might create a teenage character who is exploring various career options, someone who is having problems with the opposite sex, or an office worker caught up in office politics.

Your sample comic strips should be two to three times the size of the actual newspaper strip. On heavyweight paper, lay out your borders, rule in your lettering guide, and pencil in your drawings. Make sure your characters' dialogue runs smoothly from left to right. Follow the rest of the procedures outlined earlier in the section on magazine submissions. Ink your borders, characters, lettering, and backgrounds, and when the ink dries, erase any pencil lines. It will take at least three weeks of work to create enough material—roughly eighteen completed cartoon strips—to submit to the various syndicates (a list of the major syndicates appears in Appendix D). Put your name and phone number on each strip, and again, don't forget the self-addressed, stamped return envelope.

CONTRACTS

If you're lucky—very lucky—the syndicate may send you what is known in the trade as a development contract, which pays in the neighborhood of $2,000 to $4,000. This ties you to a given syndicate while they work with you to polish and perfect your work for syndication to newspapers all over the United States and Canada. At the end of the contract, the syndicate will decide if it wants to formalize your strip by signing you to a regular contract or to reject the strip for whatever reason.

While the contract terms will vary from one syndicate to another, the contract basically says that the syndicate will try to sell your work to as many newspapers as it can, and that you will provide it with your best work, on time. Usually income is split fifty-fifty between you and the syndicate. The total income you receive will depend on the number of papers that buy your strip and the size of each paper. Naturally, it is necessary to have the contract reviewed by a lawyer, preferably one familiar with these kinds of contracts. Contracts can be quite lengthy and full of clauses that are difficult for anyone, especially a beginner, to understand. Make sure you retain control of the characters you have created so you can license them to other markets, such as publishers of cartoon books or companies that make T-shirts, caps, balls, or any other items that could feature your cartoon characters.

FULL-LENGTH ANIMATED FEATURES: THE CREATIVE PROCESS

The creation of a full-length animated cartoon feature is an intricate, highly complex process that requires the time and efforts of many individuals in a variety of jobs. To produce a full-length animated feature lasting about an hour and a half, with its million or more individual drawings, a studio typically needs about a year and a half to produce the feature and an additional two or more years in preproduction. Let's explore the elements of the process, from the beginning.

Story Line to Storyboard

The story line is the basis for all films, live action or animated. Ideas for good stories can come from many sources. Quite often, story ideas originate with the animation crew. Experienced writers and story sketch artists are then assigned the overwhelming job of adapting a script for the cartoon medium.

The script is written and a *storyboard,* a sort of huge comic strip, is made. Commercial animation studios have developed the storyboard into a unique art form. On the storyboard, the plot is laid out in a series of pencil sketches that are mounted and pinned up in sequence on bulletin boards. Dialogue and descriptions of the scenes appear below each drawing. A typical storyboard will contain dialogue and action not shown in the renderings. Through the storyboard, the central ideas and themes are presented visually in a detailed analysis of the film's development. It discloses, for example, the characters' initial appearance and movement, detailed drawings of the backgrounds, depictions of scenes and sequences, and notes on music and sound effects. Through the storyboard, the animator tries to answer such questions as: Is the story clearly presented? Is it effectively done? What are the potential problems? By putting the basic plot on a board for everyone to see, it is hoped that new ideas and energy will be released, and that any problems will be immediately visible.

Paper Cutout Animation

Paper cutout animation uses paper figures held flat against a glass pressure plate. The animator moves the cutout pieces against backgrounds mounted on the glass. An animation camera mounted overhead takes one, two, three, and sometimes four exposures between each movement. One superb example of this technique is *The Thieving Magpie,* based on Rossini's opera and made by an Italian animator. Such animation is probably best for plots featuring a lot of physical action. It does not lend itself to stories that depend on more detailed movements, figures, and facial expressions.

Puppets

Animation of three-dimensional objects, such as puppets and geometric shapes, has long fascinated animators. Here the basic principles of single-frame movement and photography apply. The puppets themselves must be sturdy, free-standing, and have flexible body joints so that they will be able to be viewed from 360 degrees. In this form of animation, the animator must build a whole new world of minisets suitable for the story while keeping in mind such elements of the process as scale, stability, camera access, and dramatic lighting.

Claymation

The animation technique that most fully uses the power of animation may be *claymation,* or clay animation. In this technique, figures made out of clay are manipulated and moved in very small increments. The clay medium permits countless variations. Nick Park, a British animation artist, is one of the foremost exponents of the technique, having won two Oscars for his short films *Creature Comforts* and *The Wrong Trousers.* For a sequence in which one of the main characters is munching on a cracker, Park estimated it took him 288 exposures to create just twelve seconds of film.

Cel Animation

The traditional and by far the most popular form of animation is *cel animation.* This process, developed by Disney, Ub Iwerks, Max Fleischer, and other renowned animators, employs multiple layers of transparent sheets of celluloid. Through cel animation you can change a component within a scene—a single layer—without having to draw every element over again. It is easier to attain finely sketched results if only one element needs to be redrawn when a change is required. When the cels and backgrounds are completed, they are placed on a mounted animation stand and photographed.

Each cel has *exposure sheets,* also known as *bar sheets,* on which the crew records the sequence and order of various cel layers, the number of exposures given each layer, and the movements of the camera.

The Animated Feature Team

The director has the job of coordinating the production from start to finish. It is his role to time the animation action and to blend all of the elements—story, animation, dialogue, recording, color, and music—that go into the finished product. The animation writer usually creates the story, defines the characters, and begins shaping the story line and the dialogue. The storyboard artist breaks the story down into its component scenes. Once the timing is figured out and the track is analyzed, these combined elements are polished by the lead animator. At the same time, background artists produce the various backgrounds needed for the film. When the backgrounds are completed, character drawings are placed on top of them for photographing. At Disney studios, as many as 1,500 backgrounds may be required for a single feature.

Before production on the film can begin, layout artists must do extensive research. These artists must be able to visualize and illustrate settings and objects from many different viewpoints. They determine the way the characters move in relation to the backgrounds and lighting, and how the action will combine with other elements in the production.

Since layout artists design and draw guidelines for other artists, including background artists, to use in their drawings, they need considerable knowledge of what the camera can and cannot do, as well as excellent drawing skills in perspective and composition.

Live actors create the voices for each of the cartoon characters before the actual animation begins. Their vocal performances give the characters life. The recorded dialogue and song go to the animator together with a graphic chart or *reading* of each voice. This reading is shown on an *exposure sheet* which provides a written record of each drawing, frame by frame, and all instructions to the camera operators.

Usually, various animators are assigned to draw the different scenes, unless the film is very short. Directors figure the maximum action points for the drawings that will be needed to complete the film. These are drawn on paper sheets and passed on to assistant animators who fill in the drawings—known as the *in-betweens*—needed to complete a given sequence. As a rule, film travels through a 35mm projector at a speed of twenty-four frames a second. Thus the director and the animator can time the action necessary to perform each specific motion or act. For example, if a character jumps a chair in one second, the director knows that it will take twenty-four frames to animate the action, and the animator knows that it will take twenty-four drawings, if each frame is to be a new drawing. In some cases drawings may take two frames each, reducing the total number of drawings required. The animator is key to the success of the feature. He or she is responsible for moving the characters' mouths, eyes, and heads to create a range of emotional responses. In this respect, the animator is like an actor with a pencil. It is the animator who makes each character come to life, just as a live actor does.

The completed drawings are converted to cel by computer. Checkers then make sure that everything is done properly and identified. Finally, a cameraman or team of operators photographs the cels. The film editor matches pieces of exposed film to the sound track.

COMPUTERS AND TECHNOLOGY IN ANIMATION

Just how important has the computer become in the creation of animation? "Extremely important," according to Debra Kaufman, a journalist who writes extensively about the field. "In ten years," she says, "it's hard to believe how far we have come in computer animation." Prior to *Star Wars,* computers were dismissed as clumsy and unrealistic, but *Star Wars* featured a digital motion control system that produced amazing visual effects. It was just a taste of what was to come.

After his tremendous box office success, *Star Wars* producer George Lucas established his studio, Industrial Light and Magic (ILM), near San Francisco. *The Adventures of Young Sherlock Holmes* (1986) was the first film in which

ILM brought computer-generated images to life. For the first time, movie audiences saw the fantastic become real, as when the film's stained-glass knight breaks out of the two-dimensional window to come to life. ILM followed this feat with even more astonishing computer-generated special effects and graphics, creating the morphing chrome man seen in *Terminator 2*. These effects prove the power of computers to create striking and believable imagery and to seamlessly blend this imagery with live-action film. Another big step forward was *Jurassic Park,* which used computers to create living, breathing dinosaurs. It was a real challenge to create organic elements such as hair and skin with the computer. The film *Jumanji* took the digital creation of animals one step further. In this film, for the first time, we saw familiar, present-day animals like monkeys and lions look and behave as they do in life.

Even with the enormous advances in computer technology, the task of creating a lifelike computer-generated human being is extremely challenging. Says Ms. Kaufman, "Our brains are hardwired to recognize the many extreme subtleties of human behavior. Even a minor detail that is off will ruin the end result." Nevertheless, she notes, we have in recent years witnessed the digital simulation of a few humans. In *Jurassic Park,* the computer created the lawyer who was devoured by a dinosaur. And in *Batman Forever,* computers created a digital Batman with flowing cape leaping off a building. In both cases, the action was far enough away to make the illusion look real.

Computers have also enabled TV commercial producers to merge existing footage of well-known actors such as Humphrey Bogart or Gene Kelly with newly shot animated footage. This composite of real-life images and animated effects was also used successfully in *Forrest Gump* and an anniversary episode of *Star Trek: Deep Space Nine.*

How far can the computer go? Will the computer replace animators in animated films? Not according to Disney Studios. Disney films have been using computer graphics to support animation production since the early 1980s. Far from replacing the conventional animator, says Disney, the computer is merely a tool, if an indispensable one, in producing animated features—in the layout of scenes, the creation backgrounds, the planning of complex camera moves, and the production and painting of actual drawings in some scenes. Computers help produce magnificent effects that were once painstakingly drawn by hand, such as the clock scene in *The Great Mouse Detective* or the wonderful flying carpet in *Aladdin.* Computers also relieve animators of some repetitive postproduction tasks. And they are routinely used to operate both electronic and optical camera systems.

"The most important thing to understand is that computer animation is not an art form in itself, says John Lasseter, the well-known producer-animator whose *Toy Story* was a watershed in the use of computer graphics. "The computer is merely another medium within this art form, such as pencils, clay, sand, and puppets...computer animation is not accomplished any more by computers than clay animation is created by clay." Lasseter explains that every movement in an animated scene must have a reason for being. It takes an animator to apply fundamental principles such as timing, staging, flow through, and overlapping action. "I believe that *Toy Story* was the first computer-animated film to win an Academy Award because Tinny, the windup toy, managed to humorously and poignantly convey so many human emotions," he says. "All of the objects in the film have their own personalities...which serve to propel the film and to make it unforgettable." In short, says Lasseter, computer animation combines the techniques of graphic design, animation, story writing, live action, and computer science. But as with any artistic medium, the most vital element is creativity.

CAREERS IN ANIMATION PRODUCTION

Disney Feature Animation has drawn up a list of career opportunities in different production areas, all under the heading of animation. For all of these specialized fields, you must pay attention to the use of the pencil. The time you take to discipline yourself as an artist and in developing your talents, which you will then present in your portfolio, will pay off in the end. Ultimately, level of talent is Disney's prime consideration in its hiring of artists.

Visual Development Artist

The visual development artist's job is to explore a literary or musical property under consideration for adaptation as an animated film. Working with the Feature Animation Development Department, you explore various elements of film presentation to manipulate dramatic/comic story elements, plot, moods, character conflict, and place/time elements for maximum emotional effect in characterizing the story theme. Necessary qualifications include a rich imagination, a sense of caricature and design, a strong sense of color, mastery of human and animal anatomy, ability to work in various media, and skill in conceptualizing visually in a variety of animation techniques.

Story Sketch

The story sketcher's job is to visualize a film script in a series of panels somewhat like a comic strip. You should be able to quick-sketch and have a mastery of human and animal anatomy, a sense of film, and skills in design and caricature.

Layout

This position is the equivalent of live-action film's set designer. You stage every scene and camera setup through drawings. Requirements for the job include superior drawing ability, mastery of human and animal anatomy, perspective, pictorial composition, and architectural rendering talent (pencil).

Background Painter

As a background painter, you take the layout artist's drawings and translate them into color through paint. Love of painting (particularly in gouache and acrylic paints) is a must. Other important skills include drawing ability, strong color and design sense, and the ability to adapt to different styles of painting.

Character Animation

As an animator you are a creative artist able to express your ideas clearly, forcibly, and quickly with a pencil and have an understanding of the skill of linear drawing. As a beginner in this job, you should be skilled in the mechanics of drawing animals and figures in action, able to caricature not only features, but actions, emotions, and situations. Your training should include human and animal anatomy, perspective composition, quick-sketch, and figure drawing. You should in addition have solved problems in weight, balance, movement, space, and proportion. Cartooning ability is not an important consideration if you are interested in this field.

Effects Animation

If you are an effects animator, your ability to render natural and physical phenomena such as rain, fire, and water embellishes the drawn character action in each scene. Required skills include all of those noted for character animators, with the addition of an inquisitive mind and a love of drawing the elements of nature.

Computer Animation

If you would like to contribute your computer expertise to a Disney feature animated film, you must first have a strong background in drawing, painting, and design, as well as a good color sense and a mastery of classical animation techniques.

INTERVIEW: A GREETING CARD AND COMIC STRIP CARTOONIST

I was raised in Glenview, a Chicago suburb, and attended Antioch College in Ohio, where I majored in fine arts and graduated with a bachelor of arts in 1986. I had always loved cartooning, but never thought of making a career of it. I've been creating cartoons ever since grade school, and did some for our high school yearbook. In college, I also did a few political cartoons for the campus paper.

Thinking that I wanted to go to law school, I moved out to Berkeley intending to get into law school at the University of California. First, to take advantage of the lower tuition, I wanted to establish residency there. I got a job working in an office, but I hated it because I just didn't want to be cooped up in an office all day. So I quit and tried to make a living as a street vendor in Berkeley. Then I thought I would try my luck at drawing cartoons. I did that for a year or so before I was offered a job working part time as a graphic designer for a record company. Since it was an appealing offer, I moved and took the job. Even at that time, I worked hard to build my cartooning business, now my main source of income.

There are quite a few of us who create cartoons for greeting card companies. But my stuff seems to be too far-out for most greeting card companies, so I have been creating them mostly on my own for the past few years—it's been about fourteen years now. I do it all—the sales and marketing, as well as the actual production of the postcards. The business is doing fine now, and I have not had to take a secondary job for additional income for more than ten years.

In addition to creating greeting cards, I also draw a syndicated panel once a week and have written several books. I have compiled collections of my best cartoons and have had several books published to date. My stuff, like many of the gags that appear in the *New Yorker,* consists of one-panel jokes that require some thought from the reader. I also sell to magazines. Occasionally, I am in *Ms.* magazine and in a mostly cartoon magazine called *Funny Times.* I've also had panel gags appearing in *Glamour* and *New Woman.*

My time is divided evenly between my postcard business, the panel that I do weekly for syndication, and the books that I've been working on, as well as the cartoons that I submit regularly for various magazines. I have a studio where I do my drawing, and I have an office to handle my business. I also work with two part-time workers who help me draw the cartoons. I probably spend more time thinking of ideas for new cartoons, but the postcard business takes up a lot of my time. So you can see that it is quite a hodgepodge of assignments.

I would say that I am primarily self-taught. While I've always had an artistic flair, I've never gotten an artistic education. But it seems like a good many cartoonists have gone to art schools like the Art Institute in Chicago. I'm sorry that I didn't attend school there. It might have helped, because I find that your style is largely dependent on your limitations and I'm not that good an artist. I would say that in preparing for a career as a cartoonist, you need as broad an education as possible. In my own case, besides taking a lot of philosophy courses, I majored in biology because it applies to almost everything that we do in life. Training in the arts will help, obviously, although you can get by without it and many cartoonists have done just that.

A few places in the country offer specific training for cartoonists—the College of Visual Arts in New York is one—but there aren't too many. After completing college, I took a course in gags and humor and another in designing and marketing at a school in California, the California College of Arts and Crafts. Both of these courses were worth taking since they helped trim off a few years of hard knocks had I not had them. The valuable lessons I learned could have taken many years of trial and error. The cartooning course was taught by a professional gag writer and was not only informative, but also fun. He wrote jokes for a living and that was it—can you imagine? He couldn't draw at all and would sell his ideas to would-be cartoonists. The course in marketing and designing was taught by a chap who was an illustrator for Gibson Greeting cards. The two courses together provided a ton of information that you were unlikely to get on your own.

Your earnings in cartooning can vary so much that it is unbelievable. If you hit the big time with a daily strip—one taken by a major syndicator and carried in hundreds of papers across the country—and you retain the rights to all of the licensed subsidiary products based on your cartoon characters, you can earn hundreds of thousands of dollars. Consider the case of Charles Schulz, the creator of *Peanuts,* and all of the products that sport Charlie Brown, Snoopy, and Woodstock. But as you can imagine, most cartoonists earn nowhere near this kind of money. It's not the kind of field you get into expecting to earn scads of money, but it does offer a lot of personal satisfaction and that's why we do it.

Testing for your suitability for this career is kind of hit or miss. If you think your work is funny, then by all means give

it a shot. In my own case, it was mostly luck and perseverance combined. You should first of all try to get your cartoons published in as many places as possible—the high
school paper, the yearbook, and the flyers that are produced
in school. You do the same thing in college. It helps if you
can obtain some validation from your friends and class-
mates that they like your work. If no one understands what
you are trying to do, then you might as well forget about it.
Don't overlook magazines. Many magazines publish clever
gags or panel cartoons, and they are not all in the consumer
field. There are many specialty or trade magazines, such as
Linoleum Monthly, Steel Age, and so forth that use good cartoons. And there are pet magazines—such as *Cat Fancy,
Dog Fancy,* and *Bird Fancy.* Other niche magazines include
Outdoor Life, Popular Mechanics, and automobile magazines. There are dozens of these specialty magazines and
they are excellent markets for your work in various fields of
interest—sports, animals, and boats.

If you are interested in a particular aspect of cartooning—
humorous illustration, greeting cards, political cartoons—
there's a magazine for aspiring cartoonists that can be very
helpful, *Cartoonists Profiles.* It is published in Connecticut
and runs a lot of interviews with cartoonists and others in
the field, including syndicators and magazine editors. It can
be very helpful in giving you an idea of the variety of possibilities in the field. Another magazine that I love to read is
Comics Journal, which specializes in cartooning. I find it
really great to learn how other cartoonists get their ideas and

how they got started. It's really inspiring, since they come from all walks of life and all parts of the country, but they all share a fundamental belief that cartooning is something that they had to do. This was what they wanted to do and they would not be happy doing anything else.

In the future, I'd love to write some more books. Also, I'd like to branch out into children's books and perhaps do more illustrations and cartoons for magazines.

CHAPTER 4

WHAT IT TAKES TO SUCCEED

The field of cartooning and animation is not for everybody. In fact, it's not for most people. If you like a secure job with fairly regular hours and uniform work—in other words, where you know what to expect from day to day—then cartooning is probably not for you. And while the rewards can be very great, especially if your cartoon strip is syndicated and appears in hundreds of newspapers, it's a very tough field to break into. The competition is keen and few have the talent to succeed. Even talent does not automatically spell success.

THE CARTOONING ITCH

More than anything else, you must have the itch—a built-in desire to draw or cartoon—if you want to make it in the field. As John McPherson, creator of the *Close to Home* strip, puts it, "To succeed in cartooning, you have to want it bad enough." Chances are, he says, if he won the lottery, he'd still be cartooning, because he loves what he does. And chances are that McPherson's comment holds true of just about every other cartoonist. The itch to create shows itself early on, in childhood, and with it you can climb mountains. You will have the fortitude to persist no matter what. You may have to work outside the field as an illustrator for an advertising agency, doing layouts for an art studio, or as a waiter, dishwasher, or bricklayer—anything to make a living. And you may have to confine your cartooning to your spare time, including evenings and weekends. The point is that you must be so smitten with cartooning that you will do whatever it takes to succeed, for as long as it takes.

DRAWING AND WRITING TALENT

The other critical element in this equation is talent. Simply put, you must be talented in drawing. That does not mean you have to be a Michaelangelo or a Botticelli, but you have to be able to draw objects with enough realism that the reader will recognize them instantly. You must have the ability to create a cartoon that can stand pretty much on its own, with a few strategically placed words of explanation.

Most cartoonists no doubt find the drawing task the most natural part of the art. But you must also have the ability to write clearly and succinctly. Bill Amend, the creator of the comic strip *Fox Trot,* finds that the writing is the most natural aspect of creating a cartoon, so he has to spend more time with his drawing to make it reflect his message. Your writing has to be easily read and understood, and to convey your message in as little space as possible. This is not easily accomplished. *Beetle Bailey*'s Mort Walker says readers will give your strip no more than seven seconds. If it looks like it's going to be difficult to comprehend or if there are too many words, they will just skip it.

A POINT OF VIEW

You've also got to have a style that reflects who you are and how you operate. To put it another way, you've got to say what you think and not what you think the public wants you to say. You've got to be completely honest. As one cartoonist put it, cartooning is your own point of view—it's personal and reflects your personality.

To develop a point of view, you've got to be a student of human nature, understand what makes people tick, and know what's happening out there in the world—fashion, new trends, current events, and hot topics. You should read everything you can get your hands on. Keep up with the news in all of the media, including books, newspapers, magazines, and anything else that reflects what is happening in the world at large. You've got to spend time watching TV and going to movies because both of these media are a reflection of society, of the way we look, act, talk, and of what turns us on. This is the kind of material that you, as the cartoonist, must polish and transform into something that rings a bell with your audience. One cartoonist puts it this way: "Read a lot, watch a lot of TV, travel, suffer, take life-drawing classes, visit museums, find a job with a weekly newspaper, and hope for the big time. And hold on to your day job." One or two cartoonists have even suggested that a talent in drama or in acting can help, not that you have to be another Lawrence Olivier, but in terms of understanding human nature and knowing how to reach the emotions of your viewers or readers.

In addition your point of view must include a good sense of humor. Ordinarily, this is something inherent—you either have it or you don't. But by studying some of the great comedians of the past—Jack Benny, Bob Hope, George Burns, and Gracie Allen—and current stars such as Jay Leno, David Letterman, Jim Carrey, Chris Rock, and Mike Meyers, you get an idea of what their audience finds funny, what works for them and what doesn't. It may not work for you, but it's something to start with, and you can work at it until you polish your own approach to humor as reflected in your cartoons.

CHARACTER DEVELOPMENT

Charles M. Schulz says that before you do anything, you must develop some unique and outstanding characters like L'il Abner, Popeye, and Nancy. Very few people will remember the words we write, he says, but they will remember the personalities of the characters we draw and the way they looked. Characters must spring from our own personalities, our own experiences, and our own views. Often, successful comic strip characters will become more real to the reader than real life as they laugh, cry, and show emotions such as anger or contentment. Over the years, we have seen them develop and many times age, as in *Gasoline Alley* or *For Better or for Worse,* and of course in *Little Orphan Annie.*

How do we create memorable characters? Many successful cartoonists found inspiration literally in their own backyards. *Dennis the Menace* sprang into real life when cartoonist Hank Ketcham learned that his wife called their son Dennis "the menace." The characters that populate Bill Keane's *Family Circus* were all based on members of his family. Animator Walter Lantz, creator of Woody Woodpecker, modeled this famed character after a pesky woodpecker that kept bothering him and his bride during their honeymoon. "Hagar the Horrible" was the name trumped up for cartoonist Dik Browne by his sons. If you know this cartoon strip, you know that Hagar's horned helmet, rough beard, and shaggy tunic make him look somewhat like a caveman or primitive Viking, but you also know that Hagar has a soft underbelly that comes out periodically.

PERSEVERANCE

In order to succeed, you need the ability to stick with your work even when you draw a complete blank as to what you want to draw or say. This happens to just about all cartoonists at one time or another. You can't let writer's or creative block get you down. You must work your way out of this period until you are once again producing. If your strip is syndicated, you know that you have to produce a certain number of strips, as the expression goes, come hell or high water. As one syndicate executive says, "You have to produce your work week in and week out and you have to consistently turn out good work. You can't be the sort of a person where, when you experience highs, you turn out good work and then go through down periods when you have nothing to show for your efforts." Cartooning, especially comic strip cartooning, is a discipline. Often, you must work hard to get over periods when you find it difficult to generate ideas. It may take several efforts, but eventually you will be inspired and find your niche. Chic Young, the creator of *Blondie,* drew several strips that failed before he clicked with *Blondie* many years ago.

These keys to success also apply to animators.

TRAINING AND EDUCATION

What kind of schooling will help you in your quest to learn the art of cartooning? Most cartoonists agree that a broad liberal arts background is best, and, surprisingly, most caution against art school. However, if an art school also provides a broad-based liberal arts program, including music, drama, politics, science, and history, it could be very beneficial. It's a good idea to take at least one drawing course somewhere along the line, so that you can learn to draw a bit more realistically, even though cartooning is by nature exaggerated and unrealistic. Who ever saw a human with the overblown hands that characterize a cartoon character like Popeye?

Unfortunately, only one or two schools in the entire country offer formal cartooning courses (see Appendix E). Joe Kubert's School of Cartoon and Graphic Arts, in Dover, New Jersey offers a three-year program in film animation and cartooning. It is taught by respected professionals and graduates who have found jobs in comic books, syndication, and greeting cards with leading companies such as Disney Studios, Hallmark, and Marvel Comics. As one successful graduate put it, "The course load was unbelievable, but it really prepares you to meet deadlines and improves your artistic ability much more than you could do on your own. Also, even though it emphasizes comic book art, we were well trained in other areas such as the human figure, advertising, method, and materials." Another highly respected school is New York City's School of Visual Arts. Here, respected professionals have been teaching for more than forty years.

In animation, the situation is considerably different, with several schools that are highly recommended (see Appendix E). Most of these schools offer courses in both traditional and computer-assisted animation. The key to animation remains the story and the animator's ability to tell the story in a way that touches the viewer. The animator must add the elements of humor, drama, and other emotions that stir us and really strike home. But since the technical part of animation, and especially computer graphics, is so prominent today, it is strongly suggested that you enroll in a program that offers a degree in the fine arts, film or video, or animation. You need on overall idea of what is involved in the animation process, including how you account for the passage of time on film or how many frames to account for any given action of your characters. You have to be able to take a scene piece by piece and frame by frame. Understanding the parts is the formula for understanding the whole. Four-year programs are the norm, although a few are three years. Tuition can be quite high, ranging from about $10,000 to $20,000 a year, excluding room and board and books. Fortunately, most schools offer financial assistance in the form of federal and state loans, scholarships, and work–study programs. When researching these programs, you will certainly want to look into the types and levels of financial assistance offered.

While California Institute of the Arts (Cal Arts) is perhaps the most prestigious school for studying animation, it is also one of the hardest to get into. Nearly all of the schools listed in the Appendix offer the background training and technical courses you need to work in animation today, whether at one of the big Hollywood studios, such as Disney, Hanna-Barbara, or Universal, or at one of the many production studios located throughout the United States and Canada. These smaller studios do a good deal of the work for television commercials and special effects, and much more.

Keep in mind that, increasingly, community colleges are offering courses in basic animation and computer graphics and video production. To ensure a place in any of these programs, as well as the other schools listed in Appendix E, you must register early. Ordinarily, community programs offer a basic course that is more affordable and more accessible than the three- and four-year programs. The programs offered in community colleges provide an introduction to computer graphics, but you may want to consider going on to some of the other schools listed because they offer more advanced computer graphics and imaging equipment.

If you are interested in applying for a position with Disney, note that Disney and most other major studios welcome submissions from anyone in his or her final year of college or with a degree from any accredited college or university. Contact Disney Animation Training for additional details by writing to Walt Disney Feature Animation, 2100 Riverside Drive, Burbank, CA 91506.

For less formal training in animation or cartooning, try contacting a local art museum to see if it offers any cartooning courses. You might also take a correspondence course. One that is especially recommended is Cartoonerama, a twenty-four-lesson course covering every phase of cartoon art, including generating ideas and perfecting your lettering. For more information, write to Cartoonerama, P.O. Box 854, Portland, ME 04104. Many books offer lessons in cartooning and advice on getting started. Many of these even offer personal feedback on your work. They usually cover a variety of areas, including how to draw faces, bodies, hands, feet, motion, background, perspective, and a good deal more. (See Appendix A.)

What else can you do to learn something about cartooning? Obviously you should study the masters, and there is no better way to start than to subscribe to the Sunday paper and to start reading the comics every day. Read cartoon books to learn what makes these collections so successful. Read all kinds of comic books—those whose humor tends to be dark or sarcastic, like *Sylvia* by Nicole Hollander or Bud Grace's *Ernie,* or whose humor is more gentle and family-oriented, such as Lynn Johnston's *For Better or for Worse.*

INTERVIEW: A COMIC STRIP, COMIC BOOK, AND NEWSMAGAZINE ARTIST

For as long as I can remember, I always wanted to be a cartoonist. I always had the itch to follow this career. Both my grandparents worked at a paper in Kansas City, and I would often go visit them there. I was always amazed to see what the artists who worked in the art department were turning out. There was a fellow, now retired, who lived nearby, and I'd visit him. He would create some pictures to amuse me, and that too gave me the bug to get into cartooning. I remember that in grade school I would draw heavily muscled strongmen in sports and did personal strips of myself and some of my friends.

Many potential cartoonists do not go to college and wind up working for companies drawing cartoon strips just the same. I ended up in art school, at the Art Institute in Chicago, because I always liked to draw. I also took communications courses in undergraduate college at the University of Texas in Austin to help me in communicating my thoughts on the drawing board. I want to become a better storyteller and am working on a story right now. I have about ninety pages completed already.

For the past seven years or so I have been doing a weekly cartoon strip for a paper in Chicago called *New City*. It is widely distributed in many areas of the city. To my knowledge, it is the only full-color strip in what is known as the alternative press. It follows a continuing story line, which is interrupted every now and then with jokes to lighten the plot. Probably the foremost cartoonist in alternative comics is Ben Katchor, who was recently picked up by the *Village Voice,* but as far as I know, mine is the only alternative strip that appears in full color in the world.

I estimate that I put in about thirty hours a week on the cartoon strip for *New City,* and I do a lot of additional freelance work, primarily in the area of magazine illustration. My comic strip work is not like any other medium— it's something that I am thinking about constantly, if I am not directly involved in it. I can get paid anywhere from $300 to $1,200 for the same work. I receive $100 a week for the comic strip for *New City.* Most of my income comes from the magazine illustration work that I do, which pays a lot better than my comic strip work, but it varies quite a bit from week to week.

Then, too, I am doing a comic book for an alternative comic book publisher out of Seattle. It comes out three times a year, and it is, basically, a compilation of my weekly strips. The book caters to a young, yuppie kind of market, with tastes and likes quite different from the mainstream publications. For the comic book, it's hard to say just how much time I put in. A lot of my time is spent doing what you might call busywork, like reworking plots and editing.

You can probably tell that I am primarily interested in visual comic strips and not in creating gag cartoons like those that appear in the *New Yorker* and other well-known magazines. I feel pretty lucky. For one, I am doing what I want to do and nobody is censoring my work. Very few of us in cartooning are making anything like a fortune. We are, for the most part, just getting by, except for the cartoonists who make daily comic strips for syndicates.

My advice is to draw as much as you can and only what you really enjoy doing. In cartooning, you, like many others, may come to it expecting to arouse a certain emotional feeling—sympathy, laughter, fear, or whatever—but you won't succeed all the time, no matter how hard you try. You may think that you can work for greeting card companies, or draw animals or whatever, but again, I say stick to those things that appeal to you the most. In cartooning, you should not try to base your work on what readers want to see—that is the wrong way to look at it. Your work must first and foremost appeal to you. Hopefully, it will appeal to others as well. If your heart is really not in your work, it will become tiresome and very difficult.

Most of the assignments that I get are through word of mouth. I don't send out my work on speculation for editors to see. But I have done illustrations for *Entertainment Weekly, Spy,* and the *National Lampoon,* and more recently for the *New Yorker* and for the *Yale Review.* Syndication pays very well, it's true, but it's hard to accomplish. Each syndicate probably promotes two strips a year out of the hundreds that they view. Because of space limitations and the extraordinary censorship and editorial restraints, I just can't see myself working for a syndicate.

One of the hardest parts of cartooning is making your work seem authentic and avoiding situations in which your characters are not believable or are affectations of your mind. It's also very hard to take when you get an idea that you are certain will work and then realize halfway through that it won't work in any way. To my way of thinking, cartooning has to be completely creative and original—where your mind is creating the entire concept. In my class, I find myself trying to teach drawing, composition, gestures, and other concepts important to creating cartoons. All of these elements are involved in visual patterning rhythms and are part of the elements and skills that I believe you need in order to be a successful cartoonist.

INTERVIEW: A DIRECTOR OF ANIMATION IN A COLLEGE FILM DEPARTMENT

I've been here at Columbia [in Chicago] for over twenty-one years and full time for about eleven years. We're a part of the film and video department, and last semester we had 450 students in our animation program. Of those 450 students, some are taking two or three classes, so we have about 250 students majoring in animation. We are an open admissions college, which means that anyone who has a high school diploma is admitted.

When I came here we had one room, a couple of drawing desks, and a handful of kids who enjoyed animation. But since *Roger Rabbit* came out in 1988, the program has absolutely taken off because the profession is so hot. We don't advertise—it's word of mouth for our school—but we're inundated with applications from students seeking to be enrolled here.

We teach both computer animation and traditional animation. Our philosophy is that you need to be a traditional animator before you can be a computer animator, sand animator, cutout drawer, or anything else. We run our students through a very intensive two-year program that covers history, basic skills, storytelling skills, training, and motion before they actually get into studying computer animation. We don't have a master's degree at this point, although there is one in the works.

About a year ago, we moved into our new space on the seventh floor of our building. It's about six thousand square feet and next summer we are moving into a space of about twenty thousand square feet in a building down the street. Our school is growing so fast—17 to 20 percent a year—that the space we're in just can't support the number of students.

Computers have opened up a lot of possibilities in the field. There's a major misconception among students that in animation you really don't have to know how to draw. That's why they want to get into computer animation. They say, "Well, I really don't like to draw, but I like to work with computers." When I hear this, I wind up directing them to other schools because we believe that you have to be an animator before you get into computer animation. We believe that the computer is a tool, not the means itself.

Unlike most students today who grew up working with computers in some capacity or other, I had to learn as an adult how to use computers to help me with my work, and I still can't think in logical terms like computers do. Most artists think illogically. So we do the whole bit in animation: puppetry, stop motion, claymation; we do shooting through levels of glass; we do shooting with 16mm film, and we're going to be shooting through 35mm film this fall. While we used to do bucket tests, now we only do video pencil tests, which are single-frame perfect. We also have twenty-seven SGI (Silicon Graphics Incorporated) computers for high-end computer labs. We go from learning animation to applying it on the computer for many of our kids. We also jump right into working on the silicon graphics machines running Soft Image, which is a beautiful piece of software. We don't mess around. We work with all kinds of top-notch pieces of animation software.

Once the kids know the art of storytelling, storyboarding, character design, timing, sound, history, and figure drawing, then we bring them into applying those elements to an original story. In their last two years, students spend most of their time working on their own stuff and trying to get their portfolios together.

We try to balance the course work, working not just with computers but also with sand animation, clay animation, and cutouts. We try to show students the many career possibilities and then allow them to choose which one best suits their talents and interests. Other schools like Sheridan College in Toronto specifically emphasize classical animation. One of our instructors was trained there. It's a very good school for studying animation. It's also very expensive and very exclusive; they accept only a handful of students every year.

A useful listing of accredited schools is available on the Internet from awn.com. It's connected with *Animation* magazine. In our case, we don't have to go out of our way to attract students. When we start advertising, which we are going to do this fall, we're going to be swamped with applications. Everybody wants to major in animation. It's very hot, probably the entertainment part as well as CD-ROMs, CD-titles, CD-Macs. There are so many markets for graduates—television commercials, educational software. The neat thing about animation is that it's right on the cutting edge of all of these various technologies. Some of our students start here in Chicago when they first graduate, but most of them wind up on the West coast in Los Angeles or San Francisco if they are serious about a job, because that is where the major studios are located.

One of my students called me this morning. She is a junior who got an internship with Will Vinton Associates. They are one of the best stop-motion houses in the United States. And Will Vinton goes way back. I first saw his film, a piece called *Closed Mondays,* when I was just leaving graduate school. It's about an alcoholic who goes into an art museum and then experiences the artwork from tainted eyes, so the sculptures and the paintings come to life. He and Bob Gardner made the film when they were graduate students. Will Vinton has gone on to do characters for Domino's pizza and the famous singing raisins commercial. That's all Will Vinton—vintage Will Vinton. He's very successful in stop motion and computer animation. One of our animators who was with us in 1988 is one of the stop animators—Jim Richardson. He made a film here that won the Academy Award called *Cat and Rat.* He's a top animator in the industry and he's working on the yellow M&M for the M&M's commercials. He's doing it all on the computer, though he's also a terrific traditional animator.

You can take traditional animation and scan it into the computer and digitally paint it, so there's no more brushes and paints. The analogy I use for my students is that it's like an electron microscope. What can you see now that you have this wonderful, high-power microscope? You can see things that nobody has seen before. You can go places nobody has been to before. That's exactly what a computer does. You can go anywhere you want to go. For example, the electron microscope takes things like dust, and shows you the dust mites and other creatures that you can find in dust—things that we would not be aware of otherwise.

In computer animation, we can create, using mathematical processes, the real world, and then fly through it. We can go inside walls and inside watches. They are making tiny nanotechnology motors now that are about the size of a pinpoint, which may eventually be injected into your bloodstream. And the computer allows us to do things that you could never imagine. Computer photos start very large and then they are electrophotographically reduced to microscopic scale.

This only began around 1971, when the first pocket calculator came out. When I graduated from Northwestern with my master's degree, I had a storyboard for the computer that I used to do my work. At this time, we were using mainframe computers, and I didn't have access to the computers at Northwestern, so it wasn't the most technologically advanced way of working on animation. When I got to Columbia, we were teaching packaging design and animation, and I received a faculty grant to go to the Art Institute [Chicago] to learn more about computers and their uses. The Art Institute was using the Apple Alice, which was very fast. Today, it's a different world, filled with faster, more complex programs. It's absolutely incredible what's happened with software.

Our tuition falls between that of the Art Institute and city colleges—I believe it's about $300-plus per credit hour. Twelve hours per semester is full time, so the kids will pay about $4,000 to $5,000 a semester—between $8,000 and $10,000 a year. Financial aid is available to some students, and about 40 to 50 percent of the students here are receiving financial aid of some kind. Actually, when I started here in the middle seventies, we had a lot more kids that were getting federal money. Today, that money seems to have dried up and the kids are receiving local grants instead.

A high school diploma is essentially our only requirement, because, as I said before, we are an open admission college. If the kids can get a seat in a class, they can take it. We do have prerequisites beyond the basics, so we have established a beginning class that really puts these kids through the mill and makes them produce what we feel they are expected to show, not so much from a talent point of view, but to show their work habits, commitment, perseverance, responsiveness, punctuality—all things that will indicate whether you stand a chance of making it in animation.

It's a demanding niche market. When Disney made *A Bug's Life,* I believe they employed a couple of hundred animators and traditional computers. It's a field where if you have the talent and you really want to do it, the sky's the limit. Now we have several graduates who are working at Disney, and they love it. One of Disney's animators with several Disney units was a guest here recently. He brought in character studies, talked to our students, and conducted some workshops. For many kids, getting a job with Disney enables them to work anywhere. We have about twelve of our graduates working there now, mostly in production.

We have animators working at all of the major studios in town—there are about four or five major studios here. We have two producer-directors working at Warner Bros., and Jim Richardson is at Will Vinton Associates. Their staffs are made up mostly of Columbia people. At Calabash, one of the top animation houses in the United States, they create CGI (computer graphics), stop motion, cut paper, and traditional cel animation. They have some young animators who are wonderful. There is one young lady who is extremely talented. She does sand animation and just about every other aspect of the animation process.

Even with the demand for those with high-tech skills, there is still a large market for those with traditional animation skills. Similar to the predictions that the computer would cut down on the need for paper and that television was going to completely replace the radio—both of which have not yet come true—animators' talents are still necessary to the process of producing animated films. Even though computers are a necessary part of the process of creating animated features, the entertainment industry itself is really based upon your audience's likes and dislikes. Audiences get bored very easily, so you always have to be original, which means coming up with new ideas, and that can only be done with a living, breathing human being.

The major benefit of employing computers instead of manpower is that it can dramatically cut down on production time. I don't know what the cost difference is in developing a feature using computers as compared to traditional animation, but I would be surprised if there was much of a difference at all. Both ways are expensive, primarily because of the man-hours of work required to complete a job.

Disney cut down on time by using animators from overseas to handle a lot of the postproduction and by doing CAP [Computer-Aided software Programs], which now handles all of their scanning, digital inking, and painting in preparing their backgrounds.

The market is both commercially oriented and feature entertainment oriented. You really cannot separate the two. The educational market is a big one and within that market there are submarkets, including religious markets and others. There's a company in town called Big Idea Productions, and they create some animated vegetables using software. Currently they are making a feature right here in Chicago called *Computer Animation.* Their approach is based on religious values and on quotations from the Bible. Animated vegetables teach morals and lessons or "veggie tales" that are designed to spread these values. You can find licensed products, including dolls and T-shirts, based on these characters all over the place, including the megastore Sam's Club. Big Idea Productions is doing very well. One of their young men, who used to be the art director, helped to write the computer animation program because he was a teacher in our computer animation program while he was an art director there.

We have an internship office where we help to develop leads for students and this gives them a chance to receive course credit. This way they can work at the studios a semester or two, network with others active in the industry, and work on their portfolios. One of the things that students learn is that the field is very, very competitive. Talent, punctuality, solid work habits, commitment, and love of the media are traits you must possess in order to succeed. There are many easier ways to make a living. If students don't love it, they really should look for employment somewhere else.

Many of our students work full time in jobs not related to animation in order to support themselves while they freelance in their spare time. We hire many of our best and brightest students as teaching assistants, helping us run the program and keep it going. We choose them based on their track record, their attitude, and their talents and pay them to help us run the program. Hopefully, this establishes a creative atmosphere where they can work with other students in putting pieces of animation together. Then, when jobs become available, I usually consider my T.A.'s first.

About a week and a half ago, a woman called me who runs a small advertising agency. She needed a short film made and wanted to know if we had a student who could do it. So I thought of one of our students who is a terrific animator and who has been with us for a while. He is a traditional animator, but he also knows the computer. I got in touch with him, and he set up an interview with the agency. He was very impressed with the woman's presentation of the job, and, likewise, she was impressed with him. His unique character design was exactly what she was looking for, so he got the job and he loves it.

Most of the kids start at around $8 or $9 an hour—it depends on the job and how much they are needed. I know that in computer animation one of our former students now runs a shop in Milwaukee, and he was talking in the range of $40,000 to $55,000 for some of these kids to start out with. Some of it has to do with competition for talented students. When DreamWorks came on the scene, Disney had to pay more because of the competition for talented animators. Now these young animators get signing bonuses. Many of the people who work at Disney also receive residuals on the films that they work on. This is very different from the compensation in the forties, when animators didn't even get screen credit. It's a different field today.

One former student from Russia animates and creates a complete series of cartoons on the Cartoon Network called *Dexter's Laboratory*. It's a traditional animated character, which is done very well, and he farms most of his stuff to Korea or Taiwan for postproduction, because he wants it done in the traditional way. More and more often, though, studios are becoming digitally contained. We began to use digitally contained software about three years ago with a product called Toons. It was made by the same company that made Soft Image, so we knew the compatibility was there. We recently acquired USA Animation's digitally contained software and another called Animo, so we have all three programs this fall. They are high-end quaint-and-paint systems and a whole lot more, including pencil tests, final renderings, and live action. We are just getting into these, because now that we have our high-end labs established, we want to see what else we can do, so we are always looking for what the students might want to try.

To tell if you are right for cartooning you should, first of all, like drawing. There are several questions that you should ask yourself when considering this field. Have you enjoyed drawing all of your life? Did you grow up doodling on any and all pieces of paper within reach? Did you create cartoons for your high school newspaper? (In my own case, I didn't enjoy history that much, but I could summarize it in a cartoon strip.) Do you enjoy working with your hands? Do you love to be creative? Do you enjoy challenges? It's very much an individual effort until you get to the production level, and then you must be a team player. All members of the team have to pull their own weight and have the talent to make each part of the process work in order to make the whole run smoothly. The collective love for what they are doing is the bottom line.

We have about twenty-three part-time people teaching for us. Though Chicago is not a headquarters for animation, I always manage to find good instructors—people who love animation. One fellow who has been winning awards with his own personal films, who happens to be a terrific stop-motion animator, is joining our part-time faculty and freelancing to supplement his income.

It's nice working in Chicago because there are no unions. You can be self-motivated, and with a school like ours, where we have all of the equipment you need to make films, you have access to the resources to do your own thing as well as teach. That's often the reason kids come here—to get access to the equipment and to get the knowledge that they will need in operating this equipment. We give them a cursory knowledge of the equipment, but they have to apply it, even though we keep them away from the computer for the first two years. We have them think and work with their hands to give them a solid knowledge base to build on later in their schooling. We find out who can do the technical and the creative and the direction.

There is a terrific Belgian animator that I know who visited our school many years ago. When I came here, our director at the time invited me down. I was at Northwestern at the time and I remember that this Belgian chap told us that an animator is like a gardener. It doesn't happen unless you make it happen. You start from absolute zero. That garden is only going to look as good as you make it look. The creativity involved in starting from scratch is challenging and demanding. Technologically, you have to be savvy. You have to be able to change your styles constantly. Illustrators know that. Their life is three to five years. Animation involves the best of the arts—the fine arts, filmmaking, computer technology. One of our finest animators is John Lasseter, the director of *Toy Story,* whom I first ran into at a film festival in the late sixties. He was working at Disney for a while and is a great animator.

Kids are most creative. And that's what we are trying to do here—to get our students to approach things in a more childlike manner. Everyone is born with different talents, personalities, and views. We try to show our students that drawing has styles and approaches can vary. An example is Tim Burton, who's a terrific animator. But it took him ten years to get his foot in the door at Disney to make his stop-motion film *The Nightmare Before Christmas.* It's wonderful and it's different. He also did *James and the Giant Peach.* And the stop motion in both of those films is just absolutely perfect. Another extremely talented animator out of a London studio is Nick Park, who did *The Wrong Trousers.* And the images that he eventually animated were in his soul fifteen or twenty years before he did so. He's a master craftsman and has won several Oscars for his work.

CHAPTER 5

GETTING STARTED

Getting started as a cartoonist or animator isn't easy, but your options are very broad. Creating cartoons for magazines, crafting comic strips for newspapers or comic book publishers, having your comic strip syndicated, illustrating children's books, illustrating greeting cards and calendars, and working for an advertising agency are just a few possibilities for working in the cartooning field. As an animator, options include working for an advertising agency, doing animation for various production houses located throughout the United States and Canada, teaching animation either part time or full time in community colleges, art schools, and other schools of the fine and graphic arts, and working for one of the major studios, such as Disney, DreamWorks, Universal, or Warner Bros.

Very few cartoonists go right from school into a full-time job in cartooning. Most get jobs in advertising agencies or art and layout studios as illustrators or graphic arts designers, or with book and magazine publishers as illustrators and layout designers. Others start out in any number of jobs, as waiters, salespeople, and so forth—just to earn a living. They reserve their evenings, weekends, and holiday time for cartooning. If you have a husband or wife who works, you might be able to live off his or her income until you click as a cartoonist or animator.

NEWSPAPERS VS. MAGAZINES

The market for newspaper comic strips has diminished over time, and, as one cartoonist recently observed, it takes so long to get established that anyone under forty is probably working a second job or creating cartoons only in his or her spare time. You may find yourself juggling comic strips, freelance graphic arts design, editorial strips, headline design, and more. Many cartoonists recommend starting out by submitting panel cartoons or gags to magazines and special interest publications of all sorts. This is probably the best way to see if you have the thick skin necessary to withstand the rejection slips that will almost certainly come your way, especially at the beginning. This path can also be a very helpful barometer of how much you enjoy cartooning. If you attain any degree of success at this, you can go on to loftier and more demanding projects, such as pitching comic book publishers on a comic book idea, or trying your luck getting your cartoon strip syndicated. This is going to take considerably more time and energy than submitting a few panel cartoons to magazines, but the magazine market is certainly a good way to test the waters.

DEALING WITH REJECTION

As you launch your career, get used to having your work rejected. Just about all cartoonists, beginners and pros, have had their work rejected at one time or another. It could be years before you make your first sale. Remember that having your work rejected is no reflection on you. Tom Cheney, a cartoonist who has had work accepted by the *New Yorker,* the *Saturday Evening Post,* and many other publications, says, " I don't think that rejections are a valid judge of a cartoonist's work. Cartoons get rejected for thousands of trivial reasons in a market that changes like the weather." To ease the pain of rejection, Cheney always asks himself why he got into the business in the first place. His answer: "I love to draw, I love writing...and I can't think of anything else I'd rather be doing." Cheney ought to know. He spent two painful years receiving rejections until he made his first cartoon sale to the *Saturday Evening Post.* Within a year of that, he sold his first cartoon to the *New Yorker.* Soon his work was accepted by more and more magazines, until he was able to go full time as a freelancer, one of "scariest" decisions he had ever made. *Luann*'s Greg Evans started submitting cartoon strips to syndicates when he was in college, in 1970, and worked at it for fifteen years on and off until *Luann* hit in 1980. More than once, he admits, he was ready to throw in the towel, but as he puts it, "As anyone who carries the cartoon virus will tell you, you can't get rid of it. It's a lifelong affliction…"

COURTING INSPIRATION

Generating ideas is probably the hardest part of being a cartoonist or an animator. That is, it's hard to generate ideas that are fresh, meaningful, and have something to say to today's cartoon strip reader. If you were to survey a dozen of today's leading cartoonists about how and where they get their ideas—the lifeblood of their work—chances are you'd get a dozen different replies.

Tom Cheney finds that the late hours of the evening and the wee hours of the morning work best for him. This is apt to be the period when his house is the quietest and when there are the fewest interruptions. John Caldwell finds that riding an exercise bike for about forty-five minutes each morning works best for him. While he rides, he also reads the newspaper or a book or a magazine and tries to draw inspiration from something that he has picked up in the course of his reading. Bud Grace, creator of *Ernie,* likes to go for long two-hour walks every day. He claims that he's always walked to get the creative juices flowing. Plus, for someone who spends most of this time at the drawing board, it gives him some exercise. *Broom-Hilda*'s Russell Myers likes to start out reading the funnies to get him in the mood. For him, coming up with gags is not so tough; the problem is finding some subject materials upon which to hang the gag. Some cartoonists carry a small, handheld tape recorder around with them at all times and tape thoughts for gags as they think of them, day or night.

One of the most common approaches to generating ideas is to simply start writing, as *Beetle Bailey*'s Mort Walker does, and see where this will take you. For example, you could write down the word *engine* and go from there to *Indian* and then to *paleface* and so forth, until inspiration strikes. Some people doodle or sketch. Experiment with taking a simple sketch of, say, a pencil, and seeing how it can be converted into an airplane with the addition of a few simple lines. Continue this exercise in creativity until an idea pops up. Another tactic that works for many is to take another cartoonist's work and with a few deft strokes turn it into something entirely different. But the free-form principle is still the key. Take something simple, add a few lines and twists, and see where it takes you. There are many different ways you can get into the cartooning mood, many of which revolve around following a set routine every day—fishing for ideas at a certain time, day or night, exercising both body and mind, and reading daily newspapers, magazines, funnies, or comic books.

What do you do if, despite following these guidelines to the letter, you run dry or you get writer's block? This happens to all cartoonists at one time or another. You try this approach and that one, and nothing seems to work. When writer's block hits you, try to break the routine. Visit a friend, go to the aquarium or local floral gardens, watch a movie, read a book—in short, try to recharge your batteries. This should start the creative powers again.

MANY PATHS TO SUCCESS

Many successful cartoonists started out by getting published in their high school and college newspapers before hitting it big, including Bob Thaves, creator of *Frank and Ernest.* Thaves had cartoons published in his high school newspaper, then proceeded to have his cartoons published in college, then in small magazines, and gradually in larger markets. He finally succeeded, on his first try at syndication, to obtain a contract. But in his own words, "You've got to try…those who don't succeed often don't because they didn't try."

Lynn Johnston's path to success was both roundabout and long. For her first job, she worked in a Vancouver animation studio, inking and painting cels. Later, she freelanced, handling everything from typesetting to designing cereal boxes, posters, flyers, and illustrations for books. In 1972, while pregnant with her first child, she created eighty cartoons about pregnancy that were published in a book titled *David, We're Pregnant.* To her amazement, the book sold three hundred thousand copies. That was the trigger that compelled United Press Syndicate to offer her a contract on her new strip *For Better or for Worse.*

Roz Chast, one of the *New Yorker* magazine's top cartoonists, combines the careers of homemaker and cartoonist. She got her start in 1978, about a year after graduating from the Rhode Island School of Design, when several of her cartoons were picked up by a few offbeat or alternative publications like *National Lampoon* and the *Village Voice.* From there it was just a short step to the *New Yorker,* where she has been a mainstay ever since. Since then, she has had eight books of her cartoon collections published in addition to freelancing for advertising agencies and corporations.

Jerry Craft, originator of the *Mama's Boyz* strip, has attributed much of his success to a website that he himself designed. He cautions that for every overnight success in cartooning—such as *Mutts* or *Dilbert* or *Zits*—thousands are plugging along trying to hit the jackpot. Even if a syndicate doesn't offer you a contract, you should never give up. His cartoon characters are now being featured on computer mouse pads, and he is in negotiations to license his characters to several greeting card companies and animation studios.

John McPherson, the creator of *Close to Home,* worked for years as an engineer before he decided to try his hand at cartooning. After a full day at the office, he would rush home and work at cartooning well into the evening. It was a passion, an obsession that eventually paid off when he sold some of his work to a religious-oriented publication. Eventually, he was offered a contract for worldwide syndication and book rights by Universal Press Syndicate.

Jared Lee worked for years as an advertising illustrator, numbering among his clients Ralston Purina, the U.S. Postal Service, John Deere, and Sunkist. At the same time he had considerable luck in having panel cartoons accepted by such magazines as the *Saturday Evening Post, Cosmopolitan, Woman's Day,* and *Playboy.* He also created illustrations for greeting cards for Hallmark and Gibson Greetings. Eventually, in 1981, he hit pay dirt with the publication of the book *A Hippopotamus Ate the Teacher.* That was the springboard that launched him into a very successful career in children's book illustration.

As you can see, there is no one path to success in cartooning. Most likely you will have to work at a combination of tasks in the field, involving book illustration, greeting cards, comic books, and magazine gags, before you land in one of the higher-paying markets in cartooning, such as comic strip syndication or illustrating children's books. It will take a lot of work, and perhaps years of patience and a stiff upper lip, but it can be done if you have the talent and the persistence to keep trying.

WEIGHING A CARTOONING CAREER

While there is admittedly a lot of risk and little security in launching a career in cartooning, there are payoffs besides money if your strip is picked up by a syndicate. For one, you are your own boss and can determine when you want to work and what subjects you want to cover. You can be as casual as you want in your clothes and appearance, since in most cases you will work out of your own studio. And there is little if any time spent commuting to and from work. This can be a big consideration if you have a family to raise and if you are tired of the constraints of reporting in to work every day of the workweek.

On the other hand, there are the costs of setting up your own studio, investing in office furniture, computers, scanners, and everything else you will need to get started. Also, you will not be entitled to any of the job benefits that you ordinarily receive as a full-timer on a company staff, such as paid holidays and vacations, hospitalization, and life and health insurance. Unless you have a full-time job working in a related field, but not necessarily as a cartoonist, you have to pay for many job benefits on your own.

UNIQUE AND EXCITING OPPORTUNITIES IN ANIMATION

Animation is an entirely different story. If you are considering a career in animation, now is the time to act. The advent of cable and video, as well as new technology in computer graphics, has generated more animation than ever marketed to all ages. And that means more jobs, so that many more people are finding opportunities in animation.

All kinds of exciting and profitable job opportunities are opening up.

So what do you have to do to take advantage of these opportunities? For one, you need to give yourself over to your artwork completely so as to display the full range of your talents and drawing skills. You should understand that the actual job of animator covers a relatively narrow range of opportunities in the animation process. Explore the many challenging and fulfilling jobs that are part of the industry, such as layout artist, background artist, colorist, and even model builder, to see which most closely matches your skills and aptitudes. Before you even think of going out on an interview, you should have a portfolio bulging with samples of your best artwork or landscapes. If you are interested in model building, you will need to display proof of your talent in three-dimensional work. A sample storyboard or reel showing your best work is what those doing the hiring most often look for. As an alternative, you might consider making a modestly ticketed animated short and sending it to various studios you are interested in working for. You might also consider showing your animated short at one of the many film and video festivals currently thriving. You can obtain a list of such festivals from the Academy of Motion Picture Arts and Sciences.

Opportunities exist all over Canada and the United States, but one advantage of studying in a major animation capital such as Los Angeles is the multitude of internships available to students at all of the major animation studios. If you have some background in animation, this is a great way to combine some practical experience with the opportunity to make some professional contacts. While Los Angeles may have an edge in the number of internships available, good internship opportunities are to be found all over the United States and Canada. Take advantage of them. A limited number of internships, for example, are available from Walt Disney Animation Florida. Internships are described as an in-depth work experience in animation, including instruction, tutorials, practical workshops, studio assignments, and production experience. If selected, you will receive a stipend of $285 a week, covering a forty-hour workweek. Disney will also supply housing, amounting to about $77 per week, deductible from your weekly paycheck. For information regarding portfolios and résumés, contact: Walt Disney Professional Staffing, c/o Animation Division, P.O. Box 10090, Lake Buena Vista, FL 32820.

Next, you need to do some networking, which is simply an effort to widen your circle of industry acquaintances. Join various animation organizations and talk to professionals through social events or by working with them on various undertakings. And you might consider interviewing some professionals as a class project. This is another good way to get your foot in the door. Finally, explore the work of professionals who preceded you. Read everything you can about the industry. Learn about animation techniques throughout the world from the silent picture era to the present time. Some of the film festivals existing today are slanted to the avant garde or experimental films. Get to know them to learn the latest techniques influencing the industry today.

AN OPEN FIELD

Both animation and cartooning are fields that are open to anyone with talent; gender, age, and race are not barriers. Women have found the doors to success just as wide open as men. Besides Nicole Hollander and Roz Chast, among the cartoonist newcomers is Hilary Price, who at twenty-six was the youngest cartoonist in daily newspaper syndication when her strip, *Rhymes with Orange,* was launched in 1995. The strip, which deals with everything from body piercing to dating problems, now appears in more than one hundred newspapers coast to coast. Julie Larson's *The Dinette Set* started appearing in alternative newspapers in 1990 and was picked up by the King Features Syndicate six years later. Today it appears in nearly one hundred daily papers in the United States. The boom in animation and the resulting need for new talent makes that field particularly barrier-free.

EARNINGS—WHAT TO EXPECT

While the Bureau of Labor Statistics, which keeps track of earnings for various careers, does not list any figures on earnings for cartoonists and animators, an informal survey of cartoonists and animators contacted in the writing of this book revealed the following ballpark figures. There may well be wide deviations from these figures in various parts of the country, and remember that these are gross earnings from which you have to deduct such expenses as cost of advertising, computer graphics and software, business travel, and office equipment such as fax machines, photocopiers, and scanners.

As a magazine cartoonist working a few hours each night and weekends, you can earn from as little as $50 to as high as $1,000 or more a month. The higher figure would most likely be true of a seasoned professional with hundreds or thousands of cartoons in circulation. While a few magazines pay only $5 per cartoon, most pay between $50 and $500 for each single-panel cartoon published. Working full time as a magazine cartoonist, your earnings can fluctuate between $2,000 and $4,500 per month. Most magazine cartoonists supplement their incomes with earnings derived from freelancing for advertising agencies, greeting cards, calendars, children's books, and miscellaneous art for such products as mugs and T-shirts.

Illustrators doing humorous art can fit the bill of the starving artist, or earn $200,000 a year and higher. Fees paid for magazine illustrations are usually higher than those paid for cartoons, and can range from $200 for a color illustration for a small magazine to $1,500 or more for an ad agency. A greeting card illustration might earn $300, while a calendar project could pay as much as $5,000. Royalties from illustrated children's books could pay as much as several thousand dollars spread out over a few years.

Comic book artists are usually paid by the page, a sum that depends on the magazine title and the cartoonist's status. As might be expected, beginners tend to produce fewer pages per month and earn much less than pros, who work faster and produce more pages.

Full-time staff artists for greeting card companies can expect to earn between $300 and $600 a week, depending on experience, length of employment, and the size of the company.

Most political cartoonists earn roughly the same salaries as editors and reporters, which in 1998 ranged from approximately $30,000 to $60,000 a year, depending on length of service and the size of the newspaper. But if your work is sold to other newspapers by a syndicate, you can expect to earn additional royalties depending on the number and size of papers that use your cartoons.

By far the greatest earnings jackpot you can expect to hit as a newspaper strip cartoonist is syndication. Again, this market is becoming increasingly tough to crack, but if you are one of the lucky few, you can expect to see your earnings soar to between $60,000 and $150,000 a year if the strip appears in at least 300 newspapers. Unfortunately, the number of cartoonists in this bracket continues to dwindle, and several well-known cartoon strip creators continue to hold down their day jobs while devoting evenings and weekends to their strips as a protection against the possibility of having their strip canceled by the syndicate.

In the field of animation, a recent survey revealed the salaries of about forty-five job titles. A few representative titles and the median earnings of each are as follows:

Staff writer	$103,000
Producer	$208,000
Director	$109,200
Staff production board	$88,400
Art director	$153,000
Color key/color stylist	$62,500
Background layout	$91,000
Background painter	$89,400
Character animator	$106,900
Effects animator	$101,000
In-betweener	$42,300
Effects assistant	$61,200
Apprentice/trainee	$42,700

As you can see, there is quite a range between jobs, and remember, these are median figures. Many earn much less than the amounts shown, and many considerably more.

As is true of cartoonists, total earnings will reflect your experience, your status in the industry, and the size of the firm for which you work, as well as its location.

INTERVIEW: A CARTOONIST AND ILLUSTRATOR

Cartooning was something that I had dreamed of doing ever since I was a kid. I must have started around age six. I was taking pieces of paper and tearing them in half and I would make them into comic books. I started to read *MAD* magazine, and this made me want to pursue cartooning even more. In high school, I submitted work to some of the local papers and they would occasionally publish a cartoon of mine when it dealt with an issue they were interested in. I believe that I was first published at the age of fourteen. I recall that the local paper, the *Dayton Daily News,* published a series of cartoons about busing.

I went to school at St. Clair Community college in Dayton, Ohio, and came to Chicago in 1979 to attend the Art Institute until 1985. When I first came to Chicago, I started to freelance, doing artwork for small businesses and churches, and that's pretty much how I got started. I continued doing this through 1982, when I had a cartoon published in the *Chicago Defender,* Chicago's black newspaper. I built my freelancing business by going to businesses, churches, and other places that the more important artists did not want to cultivate. These were businesses that did not have a lot of money to spend, or have big budgets, but still needed artwork for whatever reason. As to the courses that I took at the Art Institute, while there was nothing directly helpful to my career, I think that the courses that I took there were very helpful in the long run. It's a very good fine arts school, which is also branching into commercial art. I took courses in animation and art education, but I believe that a general education in any liberal arts school can help in this kind of work. You should, however, take some special courses in addition to your liberal arts classes. For instance, if you want to specialize in political art, you should take some political courses.

I was interested in comic strips and fell into illustration as part of my interest in editorial cartooning. Currently I am doing editorial cartoons for mostly weekly and alternative newspapers—those that you would not consider as part of the mainstream press. In Chicago, I do cartoons for *Streetwise,* a publication widely distributed throughout the city for the homeless and people who lack shelter for one reason or another. I have appeared in *Streetwise* every week for about six or seven years now. I also have my cartoons printed in the *Madison Times Weekly,* a community paper. Mostly, the cartoons are social commentary, but they are frequently placed on the editorial pages. Right now my cartoons are appearing in about nine papers at a time. I'd like to try to get my work into some daily papers—that's my immediate objective. I've approached several syndicates about taking on my work, but have not had any luck to date. I also do a lot of graphic arts, because I have a computer setup. I can do posters, flyers, and layouts for these things. This work is important—it helps to pay for our household expenses. Currently I am dividing my time fifty-fifty between cartooning and graphic arts, but I would like to see my time being spent full time on cartooning.

The last full-time job I had was in 1985, working for a youth service agency. While there, I decided that could do better working for myself. Indeed, I did fairly well on my own. I had a lot of energy and talked to a lot of people and got them to publish several comic books—what I called social awareness books. These were distributed through the Chicago Department of Health and the Chicago Board of Education, as well as various other boards of education around the country and the local branch of the American Red Cross.

To succeed in this business, you must have a good appreciation of what is funny. You also need to have a very thick skin, because you are going to face a lot of rejection, which can be very discouraging when you are first starting out. You may think you can walk on water, but you will be brought down to earth pretty quickly in this business. I have been on the fringes of cartooning for a long time because I liked it there, but now I am part of the cartooning field in general, and I don't consider it as being hard to get into. It's just the way it worked out.

In the eighties independent comics were really big. Although today it seems that there are only a few surviving independent comics, about every ten years or so the market seems to revive. At first, you can't expect to make much money in comics, but once a comic book is established and gets into the category of *Spiderman, Batman,* and *Superman,* you can really make some money.

I would advise younger folks considering a career in cartooning to take business and accounting in high school and also to become familiar with the computer and what it can do, since you may well wind up being in business for yourself. You should also learn business writing so you can write professional, polished letters and submit cartoons to various publishers and publications.

CHAPTER 6

IN SUMMARY:
DRAWING THE FUTURE

Realistically, your chances of becoming a successful cartoonist are better if you have a day job and do cartooning on the side, or if you combine cartooning with graphic arts (lettering and layout design), designing for websites, etc. Syndication and comic books are where the big payoffs are, but both can take years of determined, hard work as a cartoonist before you make the big time, if ever. Here's how the market looks for aspiring cartoonists.

NEWSPAPER CARTOONS

The newspaper market is getting more difficult to break into. More and more metropolitan dailies are going out of business, and the number of spots open on the comics pages are dwindling as well. The same holds true of opportunities for editorial or political cartooning in the newspapers. Unless there is a dramatic rise in the number of newspapers being printed, the market for newspaper cartoonists, unsteady and dropping at best, will not look up in the near future. However, it should be noted that while the big city dailies are shrinking, suburban, weekly, and specialty newspapers are on the rise and also purchase cartoons.

COMIC BOOKS

Likewise, comic books, after a period of decline, have recently shown strong signs of surging back with the work of artists such as Alex Ross and Frank Miller. Comic books increasingly appeal to adults rather than youngsters. The opportunities for would-be comic book artists and writers look promising.

MAGAZINES

Your best bet in cartooning is to submit sample cartoons (single panel) to general consumer magazines and to the hundreds of trade or specialty magazines that also buy cartoons. Both of these markets require talent and originality. While the payoff is limited, your chances for success are much better in this market. And as noted in Chapter 3, the magazine market can be a springboard to better-paying work in a range of fields, including children's book publishing and comic books.

THE ANIMATION FAST TRACK

In animation, the signs are very encouraging. We have already shown in Chapter 1 and Chapter 3 that feature films and television shows are banking on cartoons to a degree unprecedented in modern times. Disney has risen to new heights propelled by the success of animation features such as *The Little Mermaid, The Lion King, Aladdin,* and *Tarzan.* The studio is catering to the renewed interest in animation with the release of more feature films, including *Fantasia 2000.* All of the major studios—Universal, DreamWorks, and Warner Bros.—have new animation features in the works or already released.

In television, the typical situation comedy has been pre-empted by a virtual landslide of new animated cartoons already released or on the drawing boards. This is especially true of Fox, which, based on the outstanding success of *The Simpsons* and *King of the Hill,* has three new cartoon features in its schedule. Rival networks, including Warner Bros. and UPN, also have animated shows scheduled in their lineups.

Expect to see an increased emphasis on animated commercials as well. Animation used in video games made for viewing on a television monitor or on computer screens should also show sharp increases in the near future.

A Look at Two Successful Animation Schools

As a gauge of where the animation industry is headed, consider the staggering success of Canada's Sheridan College, about a half-hour west of Toronto by train. Founded in 1968 as a fine arts college that offered a single course in traditional animation, the school now offers one of the finest college-level fine arts programs in North America, and one of the finest animation programs. Sheridan has undoubtedly had its greatest impact in the world of animation. Every year it receives 2,500 applications for the program's 110 spots. Only about half of the students complete the three-year program, which has been described as "really intense. People are dropping out all of the time because of the workload."

For those who complete the program, the rewards are worth the effort. An estimated twenty-five to forty animation studios send representatives to the school every year to review demonstration tapes and evaluate candidates for hiring. As much as a year before they graduate, Sheridan students capable of doing computer graphics on film are being offered between $50,000 to $75,000 a year. The Disney producer in charge of *The Hunchback of Notre Dame* estimates that a dozen Sheridan graduates were among the film's fifty-person animation crew.

An even more dramatic story is that of Rowland High School, located about twenty-five miles south of Hollywood's animation center. The school is home to one of the most innovative animation programs, and has quietly become the fourth-largest talent supplier to the proliferating animation industry. About fifty recent graduates now work at Disney studios, thirty at Warner Bros., and dozens at smaller production houses dotting the entire Los Angeles area. According to one recent graduate, Kim Dunning, who started at Disney for $40,000 a year, a typical entry level salary is around $40,000 per year and rapidly rises to $80,000 a year and higher. Recently, the school developed a real-time teleconferencing link with Warner Bros. Through this innovative technology, students can watch the studio's and school's training sessions.

While these success stories are perhaps a bit extreme, all animation schools are reporting enrollments at all-time highs, and similar job offers for their graduates. For all of these reasons, it is quite realistic to project that job opportunities in animation will continue to grow for qualified graduates in the years to come.

INTERVIEW: A VIDEO EDITOR
AND ANIMATION TEACHER

Besides teaching animation at the School of the Art Institute of Chicago, I also work at the museum as a video editor. I'm from St. Louis, where I attended a community college studying the fine arts. While there, I took two years of drawing, two years of figure drawing, and some sculpture in 1993 and 1994. After this, I traveled abroad to England, where I studied drawing and a little printmaking, as well as political science, history, and other courses in the liberal arts. I then transferred to the Art Institute in 1995, and I've been there ever since. After two years of undergraduate school and two years of graduate school, I took a teaching position there. When I first transferred to the Institute, I studied painting and the video arts. Eventually, I became interested in computers, and I started to study computer imaging and visualization. I ended up working with computer animation in the arts and technology departments at the Art Institute.

Currently, there isn't a separate department for computerized animation, but there is a film department that produces traditional animation and an art and technology department for computer animation. Right now the animation produced at the Institute is divided between the two departments. In the future, it may become a department of its own, but that remains to be seen. I've been working on the computer part of animation, and, while I don't have the traditional computer training for animation, what I do have is some training in film and video. My strengths are probably in editing and in computer animation, but not necessarily in character animation. I'm teaching some programming courses that focus on interactive CD-ROMS, interactive multimedia, and interactive programs for the Web. I am also teaching 3-D animation courses in which we use computers to construct three-dimensional spaces with three-dimensional characters. We make wonderful and fantastic narratives and stories.

Since the Institute is an art school, many of the students are doing things that they could not attempt to do if they were working for a large company. Many have no intention of having their work produced in a commercial manner, but they do try to enter their work in various competitions and national and international screenings. A great example is SIGGARAOH, which is an international computer graphics conference held in Los Angeles, New Orleans, and Florida. If you are looking for an animation job, this is the place to post your résumé as well as a great place to meet and network with other animators. This organization comprises producers and artists, all of whom pay a membership fee to belong—so it's part fine art and part commercial, kind of like a trade show that has a fine arts aspect to it.

In working with students, I try to find out what's on their minds, what they would like to do, what they are curious about, what experiences they have had, and what's moving them at the moment. Hopefully, by the end of the course, they've made a short that has some personal meaning to them. These short pieces vary in content and theme—some are cartoonlike and some are abstract art. I teach three classes per semester, each with about ten to twelve students, so in a semester I am usually working with thirty to thirty-six students.

I had a friend who once went for an interview at a law firm. At the time, he was working for a service that produced animation for law firms. For example, his services might be needed if the law firm was handling a case in which a plane or train crashed and they wanted an animated reconstruction of the event to show how it happened and who was at fault. The salary was in the area of $80,000. This kind of animation is done to reconstruct a variety of events without using real people or objects.

I have several other friends who work for production houses. They take jobs from advertising agencies and do various things like making thirty-second commercials. For example, the job might be for Meineke mufflers, so they are hired to animate the characters, making a muffler dance around car batteries.

One production house is called Tricky Pictures. It's a small house and they do a lot of creative work. They have many young people working there. They mix a lot of mediums, so they have pastels, they use streaming computer graphics, and they mix in some stop-motion animation. In stop-motion animation, you take a camera and create an exposure. Then you move the object and create another camera exposure, and you repeat this process over and over.

I did some freelance editing for another studio called Essential Pictures. They do character animation for short, thirty-second TV commercials. It is the job of the animation studio to know exactly what the agency is looking for in terms of content, character, and the look of the animation. Before they actually produce the animation, these companies create drawings and audio in order to illustrate the commercial's content. While working with this company, I edited some of the rough commercials together trying to figure out what the timing would be.

There's another studio called Skyview in a high rise apartment building near Essential Pictures. It's a huge production company, and they do both big and small projects. They have some powerful computers and high-end facilities, and they produce commercials for many large companies like Chevrolet. Sometimes they do creative work, but mostly they are filling in on work that has already been done by the advertising agency. There's something called a *dope sheet* that charts timing for the project, and most times it is the producer or director's job to fill this out. After you do this for a while, you can estimate the exact timing of the animated project. You then fill out the dope sheet, basically a graph of time and the placement of each image at that particular moment. An animator takes the storyboard, which has the dialogue and the main picture, and the dope sheet, which maps out the time, and uses these to create animation that conforms precisely to the producer's expectations.

The editing that I do requires a lot of thinking and conceptualization. I'm really involved in the production, but I do my own work at home so that I can do my own animations. I create them at home and send them off to international festivals. I've entered eight or nine in the past couple of years and had my work shown in several countries, including the United Kingdom, Brazil, Japan, and others.

Besides working for all of these studios, I serve as an internship supervisor. In this position, I go to the studios and talk to the animators, students, and supervisors about what they are doing on a day-to-day basis. Many times the students do very well with these internships. They can, as a result, find a job afterward as a freelancer, and eventually they move up in the company. We have internships at some of the cable outlets, but, because of union issues, not at the major TV studios.

I've heard of freelance jobs at the *Oprah* show where you are making the animations that go between the interviews. These jobs pay extremely well—up to $80 to $90 an hour. The people who fill these positions are trained or have developed skills in what we call *after effects,* which is basically two-dimensional text and video, moving around and making tiny spots for between interviews.

I've had about three or four students who have gone on to Disney Studios, and they usually start at about $35,000 a year. One drawback, though, is that they have to work six days a week, and some days they work long hours. Also, even though it seems like a very good salary, when you think about living in L.A. and the hours required for the job, it may not be quite as good as you thought. The good part is that you get a sense of how Disney works, and this can provide valuable job experience.

Large museums are also starting to make their own in-house productions. What they do is take high-resolution digital images of the artwork, the paintings, and the sculptures in order to make animations. Instead of bringing a camera into the gallery and trying to take pictures so that they are perfectly sharp and stop just right, we can now use a computer to move the pictures about and make them appear as we want them to. As the narrators are speaking, we can zoom in and out, do color corrections, do dissolves between pictures, even show the original drawings. We can use the computer to do everything that a camera can do, only more easily, quickly, and inexpensively.

Computers are very useful in many different phases of the production process, including editing and sound, for speeding up a shot, and for keeping things in order. That's what makes today's animation so incredible. In one computer application, we feed the drawing outlines to a computer, which can then quickly fill in the drawings, instead of hand-painting all of the figures. We just got the equipment that will give us the capability to do this. Or let's say you have shot A, B, C, D. With the right computer equipment and technology, you can reorder them quickly so that they now are C, A, B, D. Many producers know exactly what they want and can conceive of these shots in advance, but there's a whole new generation of people who like to experiment and flip around shots. Sometimes I talk to filmmakers who actually cut the film and splice it together. In their job, you don't really change your mind once you've made a decision. You've got to make firm decisions when you're in that position. A lot of this technology is changing the way animation is created. In one way, it's making people less decisive.

I have learned most of my computer knowledge within the past year or two because it's a developing technology. We've been upgrading our equipment rapidly, so once you get into a production studio, it's not like you're trained and you can keep doing it. It changes from year to year. We've been involved in four different programs on this job in the last three years, so you're constantly training to keep up with the technology. I would say that about 30 to 40 percent of my job is keeping up-to-date on the computer software and learning what it can do.

Also, the hours in this work are irregular. Sometimes they are simply nine to five, but many times they are not. I work here three days and I teach three days. I work six days a week trying to get a lot of experience in various assignments working with various production studios and learning the equipment. I get home, eat dinner, and perhaps get in an hour or two of work preparing for class. I have a personal computer, so I can do some imaging work and I can do some of the animation, but not the entire thing since my computer isn't sophisticated enough.

As for salaries, when you are starting, right out of school, you should expect to make somewhere around $14 an hour. If you're talented, really know the applications, and pick up things quickly, you might be able to make $30 an hour. When the students finish here, they start out with a studio and they have to be retrained into that studio's procedures. You don't have to go back to school, but each job is a little different and involves a period of learning the ropes. It might take a week or two to get used to each job and to learn the vocabulary at that particular studio.

Right now there six very powerful 3-D computer animation programs and no animator can know all of them. Some job listings may call for animators with skill in one particular kind of software, and many times your employer will change from one program to another, so you have to be flexible since it's almost impossible to train for a specific computer animation job. All we can do is provide the basic skills in computer operation and you go from there.

APPENDIX A

BIBLIOGRAPHY

NEWSPAPER AND MAGAZINE ARTICLES

Brennan, Patricia, "CBS Puts the Old in the New," *The Washington Post,* May 10, 1998.

Coburn, Marcia Froelke, "The Luck of the Draw," *Chicago* Magazine, January 1995, pp. 27–30.

Corliss, Richard, "Cartoons are No Laughing Matter," *Time* Magazine, May 12, 1997, pp. 78–80.

Craft, Jerry, "Interview," *Cartooniverse,* July 16, 1999.

Donnelly, Kathleen, "Cartoonist Nicole Hollander's Alter Ego is the Brassy Sylvia," Knight-Ridder/Tribune News Service, March 8, 1995.

Dretzka, Gary, "Redefining Animation: The Making of the Prince," *Tempo* section, *Chicago Tribune,* December 13, 1998, p. 1.

Ellin, Harlene, "Telling Tales: Newest Stable of Animal Movies Carries on Tradition Reflecting Society," *Tempo* section, *Chicago Tribune,* p. 5.

Fine, Marshall, "Animated Talk with Cartoonist," *Chicago Sun-Times,* p. 12.

Ginsburg, Janet, "Drawn from Life," *Tempo* section, *Chicago Tribune,* p. 1.

Grossmann, John, "The World According to Roz Chast," *American Way,* American Airlines, June 1, 1997, p. 65.

Hornblower, Margot, "Comic N the Hood," *Time* Magazine, July 5, 1999.

Juddery, Mark, "Pow! Comic Opportunities," *Writer's Digest,* April 1997, p. 38.

Krantz, Michael, "Animators, Sharpen Your Pixels," *Time* Magazine, November 30, 1998, pp. 109–110.

Krantz, Michael, "FOX Gets Super Animated," *Time* Magazine, January 11, 1999, pp. 92–94.

Leroux, Charles, "The Dinette Set Is Moving In," *Tempo* section, *Chicago Tribune,* July 26, 1999, p. 1.

May, Larry, "Walt Disney: Movie Maker and Entertainment Industry Entrepreneur," *The Reader's Companion to American History,* 1991 edition, p. 286.

Musgrove, Mike, "It's So Graphic," *Book World, The Washington Post,* July 26, 1998, p. 1.

Nessel, Jen, "Made in Prague, Bound for the U.S.," *The New York Times,* August 9, 1998, Section 2, p. 22.

Petrakis, John, "Animation Fest: A Taste of Simple Art and Wackiness," Movies section, *Chicago Tribune,* p. 1.

Plotkin, Hal, "Hollywood Lures High School Animators with Sweet Deals," *Inc.,* January 1997, vol. 19, p. 20.

"Pluck of the Draw," *People Weekly,* September 23, 1996, p. 78.

Protzman, Ferdinand, "The Draw of Cartoons," *The Washington Post,* August 23, 1997, p. F 2:1.

Rotenberk, Lori, "Making Her Mark," *Chicago Sun-Times,* July 9, 1997, p. 23.

Webber, Brad, "Pop Goes the Comics," Friday section, *Chicago Tribune,* July 9, 1999, p. 1.

Weller, Sam, "Alex Ross's Art Takes the Graphic Industry to New Heights," *Tempo* section, *Chicago Tribune,* July 13, 1999, p. 2.

Wood, Christopher, "The Making of a 'Toon College," *Maclean's,* vol. 109, June 24, 1996, p. 43.

Youngman, Owen, "Drawing Conclusions," *Tempo* section, *Chicago Tribune,* January 30, 1995, p. 1.

BOOKS ON CARTOONING

Becker, Stephen, *Comic Art in America.* New York: Simon & Schuster, 1959.

Bergen, Arthur Asa, *The Comic Stripped American.* New York: Walker & Co., 1973.

Ericcson, Mary Kentra, *Morrie Turner, Creator of Wee Pals.* Chicago: Children's Press, 1986.

Gerberg, Mort, *Cartooning: The Art and the Business.* New York: W. Morrow, 1989.

Glasbergen, Randy, *How to Be a Successful Cartoonist.* Cincinnati: North Light Books, 1996.

Glubok, Shirley, *The Art of the Comic Strip.* New York: Macmillan, 1979.

Goulart, Ron, *The Encyclopedia of American Comics.* New York: Promised Land/Facts on File.

Hess, Stephen, *Drawn and Quartered.* Montgomery, AL: Elliott & Clark, 1996.

Johnson, Rheta Grimsley, *Good Grief: The Story of Charles M. Schulz.* New York: Pharos Books, 1989.

Mascola, Marilyn, *Charles Schulz: Great Cartoonist.* Vero Beach, FL: Rourke Enterprises, 1989.

McCloud, Scott, *Understanding Comics.* Northampton, MA: Tundra Publishing, 1993.

Nordling, Lee, *Your Career in the Comics.* Kansas City: Andrews & McMeel, 1995.

O'Neill, Dan, and Marian O'Neill, *The Big Yellow Drawing Book.* Hugh O'Neill and Associates, 1974.

O'Sullivan, Judith, *The Great American Comic Strip: 100 Years of Cartoon Art.* Boston: Bullfinch Press, Little Brown & Company, 1990.

Richardson, John Adkins, *The Complete Book of Cartooning.* New York: Prentice Hall, 1977.

Robinson, Jerry, *The Comics: An Illustrated History of the Comic Strip.* New York: G. P. Putnam's Sons, 1974.

Tatchell, Judy, *How to Draw Cartoons and Caricatures.* Tulsa, OK: EDC, 1987.

Thomson, Ross, and Bill Hewison, *How to Draw and Sell Cartoons.* United Kingdom: North Light, 1985.

Tollison, Hal, *Cartoon Fun.* Tustin, CA: W. Foster Publishing, 1989.

Walker, Mort, and Bill Janoch, *The National Cartoonists Society Album, '88.* Raleigh, NC: Wendy Little, Olson Management.

Waugh, Colton, *The Comics.* New York: Macmillan, 1947.

BOOKS ON ANIMATION

Adams, Lee, *Animation Programming, 1st Edition.* Blue Ridge Summit, PA: Windcrest, 1993.

Andersen, Yvonne, *Make Your Own Animated Movies and Videotapes.* Boston: Little Brown & Company, 1991.

Bailey, Adrian, *Walt Disney's World of Fantasy.* New York: Everest House, 1982.

Cleave, Alan, *Cartoon Animation for Everyone.* New York: Fountain Press, 1973.

Grush, Byron, *The Shoestring Animator.* Chicago: Contemporary Books, 1981.

Halas, John, *The Technique of Film Animation.* New York: Hastings House, 1976.

Hamilton, Jake, *Special Effects in Film and Television.* New York: DK Publishing, 1998.

Hobson, Andrew, *Film Animation as a Hobby.* New York: Sterling Publishing Co., 1975.

Jenkins, Patrick, *Animation: How to Draw Your Own Flipbooks and Other Ways to Make Cartoons Move.* Reading, MA: Addison Wesley Publishing Co., 1991.

Kinsey, Anthony, *How to Make Animated Movies.* New York: Viking Press, 1970.

Laybourne, Kit, *The Animation Book: A Complete Guide to Animated Filmmaking.* New York: Crown Publishers, 1979.

Locke, Lafe, *Film Animation Technique: A Beginner's Guide and Handbook.* Whitehall, VA: 1992.

Nardo, Don, *Animation Drawings Spring to Life.* San Diego, CA: Lucen Books, 1992.

Pintoff, Ernest, *Animation 101.* Studio City, CA: Michael Wiese Productions, 1998.

Rubin, Susan, *Animation: The Art and the Industry.* Englewood Cliffs, NJ: Prentice Hall, 1984.

Schroeder, Russell K., *Walt Disney's Mickey Mouse: My Life in Pictures.* New York: Disney Press, 1997.

Walt Disney Animated Features and Silly Symphonies. New York: Abbeville Press, 1980.

Disney Feature Animation has published quite a few books on animation, some of which are listed below. For information about these, contact:

Walt Disney Feature Animation
2100 Riverside Drive
Burbank, CA 91506

Aladdin: The Making of an Animated Film, by John Culhane, 1992.

The Art of Mickey Mouse, by Craig Yoe, 1991.

The Art of Walt Disney, by Christopher Finch, 1993.

Bambi: The Story & the Film, by Ollie Johnson and Frank Thomas, 1990.

Disney Animation: The Illusion of Life, by Ollie Johnson and Frank Thomas, 1981.

The Disney Touch, by Ron Grover, 1991.

Encyclopedia of Disney Animated Characters, by John Grant, 1992.

The Man Behind the Magic: The Story of Walt Disney, by Katherine and Richard Greene, 1991.

Too Funny for Words, by Ollie Johnson and Frank Thomas.

Treasures of Disney's Animation Art, by John Canemaker, 1982.

The Ultimate Disney Trivia Book, by Kevin Neary and Dave Smith, 1992.

Walt Disney's World of Fantasy, by Leonard Maltin, 1984.

BOOKS ON PRODUCTION TECHNIQUES

Also from Disney Feature Animation:

Animation from Script to Screen, by Shamus Culhane, 1988.
The Animator's Workbook, by Tony White, 1986.
Cartoon Animation: Introduction to a Career, by Milton Gray, 1991.
The Complete Kodak Animation Book, by Charles Solomon and Ron
   Stark, 1983.
How to Create Animation, by John Cawley and Jim Korkis, 1990.
How to Draw Animation Storyboards, by Bob Singer, 1992.
Scriptwriting for Animation, by Stan Hayward, 1977.
Timing for Animation, by Harold Whitaker and John Halas, 1981.

ORGANIZATIONS

CARTOONIST ORGANIZATIONS

Comic Art Professional Society
P.O. Box 1440
Burbank, CA 91507

National Cartoonists Society
c/o Wendy Little, Olson Management
4101 Lake Boone Trail, Suite 201
Raleigh, NC 27607

Southern California Cartoonists Society
c/o Dick McIntire, Treasurer/Membership Director
5360 Oakleaf Point
San Diego, CA 92124

ANIMATION ORGANIZATIONS

ASIFA-East (New York)
  c/o Jim Petropoulos
  10 Pint Crescent
  Whitestone, NY 11357
  (718) 746-3981
  E-mail: Linda Simensky, linda.simensky@turner.com

ASIFA Central
  c/o Donna Morse
  School of Communications, Lake Superior Hall
  Grand Valley State University
  Allendale, MI 49402
  (616) 895-3101
  E-mail: Deanna Morse, asifa@asifa.org

ASIFA Canada (Vancouver)
  Case Postale 5226
  St. Laurent, Quebec
  Canada H4L 4Z8
  E-mail: Leslie Bishko, bishko@cs.sfu.ca

ASIFA Croatia (Zagreb)
  Borivoj Dovnikovic
  Hrvatskog Proljessa 36
  41040 Zagreb, Croatia
  E-mail: asifa@samson.hivolda.no

The Cartoon Arts Network
  Cartoon Arts Network Administration
  Federated Communications Ltd.
  9–10 Jew Street
  Brighton, England BN1 1UT
  (44) 1273-4705

International Animated Film Society
725 S. Victory
Burbank, CA 91502
(818) 842-8330
E-mail: Antran Manoogian, infor@asifa-hollywood.org

Magical Moments & Memories
91 Rowan Way
Exwick, Exeter
Devon, England EX4 2DT
(44) 01393-431653

PERIODICALS

Animation Journal
  AJ Press
  2011 Kingsboro Circle
  Tustin, CA 92680-6733
  E-mail: Maureen Furniss, furniss@nexus.chapman.edu

Animation Magazine
  30101 Agoura Court, Suite 110
  Agoura Hills, CA 91301-4301
  (818) 991-2884
  E-mail: animag.@aol.com

Animation World Magazine
  6525 Sunset Boulevard
  Garden Suite 10
  Hollywood, CA 90028
  E-mail: editor@awn.com

Animato Magazine
  92 Thayer Road
  Monson, MA 01057
  (413) 596-3046
  E-mail: animato22@aol.com

The Artist's Magazine
   1507 Dana Avenue
   Cincinnati, OH 45207

The Aspiring Cartoonist
   P.O. Box 18679
   Indianapolis, IN 46218

Cartoonist Profiles
   P.O. Box 325
   Fairfield, CT 06430

The Comic Buyer's Guide
   Maggie Thompson, Editor
   700 E. State Street
   Iola, WI 54990-0012

The Comics Journal
   Gary Groth, Editor
   7563 Lake City Way NE
   Seattle, WA 98115

Comic Relief
   Michael A. Kunz, Editor
   P.O. Box 6606
   Eureka, CA 95502

FPS Magazine of Animation
   Pawn Press
   P.O. Box 355, Station H
   Montreal, Quebec
   Canada H3G 2L1
   E-mail: Emru Townsend, emru@cam.org

Gag Recap
   12 Hedden Place
   New Providence, NJ 07974

In Toon Magazine
   P.O. Box 487
   White Plains, NY 10603

Persistence of Vision Magazine
   Walt's World Publishing
   3136 S. 3200 West
   Salt Lake City, UT 84119
   E-mail: Matt Crandall, matt@alumni.cal tech.edu

MAJOR NEWSPAPER SYNDICATES

For specific requirements on submitting cartoon panels or strips, write to each syndicate to request its guidelines for submission of cartoons.

Chronicle Features
870 Market Street
San Francisco, CA 94102
(415) 777-7212

Creators Syndicate
5777 W. Century Boulevard, Suite 700
Los Angeles, CA 90045
(213) 337-7003

King Features Syndicate Group
235 E. 45th Street
New York, NY 10017
(800) 526-KING, (212) 455-4000

Los Angeles Times Syndicate
218 S. Spring Street
Los Angeles, CA 90012
(213) 237-5485

Tribune Media Services
  64 E. Concord Street
  Orlando, FL 32801-1392
  (800) 245-6536, (407) 839-5600

United Media
  200 Park Avenue
  New York, NY 10166
  (800) 221-4816, (212) 692-3700

Universal Press Syndicate
  4900 Main Street
  Kansas City, MO 64112
  (800) 255-6734, (816) 932-6600

The Washington Post Writers Group
  1150 15th Street NW
  Washington, DC 20071-9200
  (800) 879-9794, (202) 334-6375

SCHOOLS

Since schedules, courses, and requirements are subject to change, it is suggested that you contact any school in which you are interested early, to get the most up-to-date information.

CARTOONING SCHOOLS

Joe Kubert School of Cartoon and Graphic Art
37 Myrtle Avenue
Dover, NJ 07801

School of Visual Arts
209 E. 23rd Street
New York, NY 10010

ANIMATION SCHOOLS

California College of Arts and Crafts
5275 Broadway
Oakland, CA 94618-1487
(510) 653-8118

California Institute of the Arts (Cal Arts)
McBean Parkway
Valencia, CA 91355
(805) 253-7825

Columbia College
600 S. Michigan Avenue
Chicago, IL 60605-1996
(312) 663-1600

Northwest Film Center
Portland Art Museum
1219 SW Park Avenue
Portland, OR 97205
(503) 221-1156

Pratt Institute
200 Willoughby Avenue
Brooklyn, NY 11205
(718) 636-3600

Rhode Island School of Design
Two College Street
Providence, RI 02903-2791
(401) 454-6100

Ringling School of Art and Design
Sarasota, FL 34234
(813) 351-4614

San Francisco Art Institute
Chestnut Street
San Francisco, CA 94133
(415) 771-7020

Savannah College of Art and Design
342 Bull Street
Savannah, GA 31401-3136
(912) 238-2400

School of the Art Institute of Chicago
37 S. Wabash Avenue
Chicago, IL 60603-3103

School of Visual Arts
209 E. 23rd Street
New York, NY 10010
(212) 592-2100

Syracuse University
Syracuse, NY 13244
(315) 443-1033

University of California at Los Angeles
405 Highland Avenue
Los Angeles, CA 90024
(310) 825-4321

University of Central Florida
4000 Central Florida Boulevard
Orlando, FL 23816
(407) 823-2000

University of Southern California
University Park
Los Angeles, CA 90089-2111
(213) 740-2311, (312) 899-5219